Connecting with
Traditional Literature

her paper. When she has finished, the students quietly begin discussing the student's paper and offering suggestions for improvement.

In this first scenario, the student is informally presenting her draft by reading aloud to two of her peers, who listen attentively. When she has finished, the others ask her questions regarding her paper. Therefore, reading is utilized as a tool to initiate the interaction between the students, and speaking and listening became tools they used to critique and offer suggestions.

A student is sitting at his desk writing quietly. He stops what he is doing, begins to erase something on the paper, then stops. As he examines the paper, his lips move quietly as he begins to read what he has written so far. He begins to write again, then rereads in a soft voice the changes he has made. Appearing satisfied, the boy continues writing.

The second scenario provides an example of how one student engages in multiple processes as a means of monitoring his own progress. As he writes, he continuously rereads, makes changes, rewrites, and reads aloud, listening to what he has written, until he is satisfied with what he has written.

Two students are working together on a character shield they have decided to do for the character Jess in Bridge to Terabithia. *As they make a list of possibilities to include about Jess on the character shield, they keep returning to the book. With heads bent over the book together, they flip through the pages until they find what they are looking for, then they begin adding more to their list of ideas. When they are satisfied they have enough, they begin to draw their character shield and fill in the information they consider to be most important.*

The third scenario shows how two students use the book they have been reading in class as the connection between what they know about Jess and what they would like to share about Jess with others. They use their reading of the book as a way to explore, investigate, confirm, and validate their ideas. Once they are satisfied with the information they have listed, they begin to make a visual representation of their ideas to present and share with the rest of the class.

All three of these scenarios illustrate how the language arts interact as students seek to initiate, develop, and monitor their literacy learning. Throughout this book, the activities we review will not only emphasize connections between reading and writing, but will also reflect how all aspects of language, listening, speaking, reading, writing, viewing, and visually representing work together to help students accomplish these goals.

LISTENING

Although basic to classroom instruction, it is questionable how often students truly listen. When a good majority of their day is spent listening, they begin to tune out and direct their attention elsewhere. Routman (1991) shares how the students she has worked with did not always listen carefully when comments were directed to the teacher by other students. When the students began participating in literature discussion groups, they were encouraged to direct their comments to each other, and, as a result, the students began to value listening to each other.

It is important for students to understand how significant the skill of learning is, and that the teacher, not just them, is a listener, too. In order for the students to understand what is meant by truly listening to each other, they must be taught. Modeling by the teacher is a great place to begin. Atwell (1987) uses *group share*, another means for helping writers improve their writing, to model for the entire group ways of listening to the writer. It involves the teacher modeling to the whole group ways that the students can listen and

Related Titles of Interest

**Connecting Informational Children's Books with
Content Area Learning**
Evelyn B. Freeman and Diane Goetz Person
ISBN: 0-205-26753-X

Best Books for Beginning Readers
Thomas G. Gunning
ISBN: 0-205-26784-X

Essentials of Children's Literature, Third Edition
Carol Lynch-Brown and Carl M. Tomlinson
ISBN: 0-205-28136-2

The Right Book, The Right Time: Helping Children Cope
Martha C. Grindler, Beverly D. Stratton, and Michael C. McKenna
ISBN: 0-205-17272-5

**Children's Books in Children's Hands: An Introduction
to Their Literature**
Charles Temple, Miriam Martinez, Junko Yokota, and Alice Naylor
ISBN: 0-205-16995-3

For more information or to purchase a book,
please call 1-800-278-3525

Connecting with Traditional Literature

Using Folktales, Fables, and Legends to Strengthen Students' Reading and Writing

Kimberly Kimbell-Lopez
Louisiana Tech University

Allyn and Bacon

Boston   London   Toronto   Sydney   Tokyo   Singapore

To
Paul, Reghan, and Kendall

Series editor: Virginia Lanigan
Series editorial assistant: Bridget Keane
Manufacturing buyer: Suzanne Lareau

Copyright © 1999 by Allyn & Bacon
A Viacom Company
Needham Heights, MA 02494

Internet: www.abacon.com

Library of Congress Cataloging-in-Publication Data

Kimbell-Lopez, Kimberly.
  Connecting with traditional literature : using folktales, fables, and legends to strengthen students' reading and writing / Kimberly Kimbell-Lopez.
     p.   cm.
  Includes bibliographical references and index.
  ISBN 0-205-27531-1
  1. Tales--Study and teaching.   2. Fables--Study and teaching.
  3. English language--Composition and exercises--Study and teaching.
  4. Reading.   I. Title.
  LB1575.K55   1999
  372.64--dc21   98-39351
                                                                        CIP

Printed in the United States of America
10 9 8 7 6 5 4 3 2 1   02 01 00 99 98

Contents

Preface

Invariably after discussing how to organize and plan for instruction using the reading and writing workshop as a model, a comment I often hear from my students and teachers is, "Yes, that sounds great, but how do I really do it?" This book, one response to that question, is designed to be a concise user-friendly resource to aid in connecting reading and writing in the classroom through the study of the genres of traditional literature. It is my goal to provide teachers with a starting point: (1) This is how I start, (2) These are things I can do, and (3) This is how I can connect the learning my students do within "self" and the learning they do with each other.

Overview of the Book

Chapter 1 covers aspects of the reading-writing connection. Chapter 2 discusses the beginning stages of introducing the different genres of study by reviewing the format of the chapters to follow. Chapters 3, 4, and 5 each begin with reviewing characteristics of a genre, sharing lesson ideas that help students study the characteristics, and then covering stages of the writing process with corresponding activities. Therefore, the major purpose of Chapters 3, 4, and 5 is to provide a discussion of the characteristics and representative stories most common to each genre.

Special features interspersed throughout the book include:

- The approaches discussed show the continuous use of reading and writing as a tool for developing individual literacies.
- Practical examples, projects, activities, reflective questions, as well as charts, diagrams, and other graphics will assist in providing a blueprint for successful learning within the community of learners.
- Social interaction between peers and teachers is emphasized.
- The use of critical thinking activities as a tool for analysis of the genre will assist in determining common characteristics. Teachers are shown how students are invited to explore and investigate commonalities across genres.
- An explanation is given on how the characteristics can be used as a mediation tool to connect reading and writing. By examining the characteristics through reading, students can construct together the framework necessary to write successfully within the genre.
- A sampling of projects and activities can serve as the springboard between reading and writing. Teachers are encouraged to select activities, projects, and literature that are most appropriate for the needs and abilities of a variety of students in their classrooms.

▓ The activities are representative of different stages of the writing process. Critical to the success of classroom instruction is how to structure it so that students are able to experiment with the various stages of writing. The purpose here is to show the natural flow that readers and writers follow as they proceed through this process.

▓ Technology connections are discussed at the end of Chapters 3, 4, and 5. These ideas relate to ways students and teachers can use technology in their study of the different genres. The suggestions range from projects involving word-processing programs, publishing programs, presentation programs, database programs, and multimedia presentation programs.

▓ References to an annotated bibliography of books for each genre are discussed.

My rationale for providing teachers with these elements, ideas, and activities is that it enables them to more effectively connect reading and writing processes utilizing a workshop format. Students in the classroom community work together to look for the characteristics within the literature by using the critical thinking and reading activities. They then write their own stories by using the guidelines first utilized to study the genre. Most important, the activities discussed are not meant to be restricted to one particular genre. They can easily be selected from and interspersed throughout a study of other genres.

Acknowledgments

I will always be grateful for having the opportunity to work with another new teacher during my first year of teaching. Deanna was my lifeline and savior for my first two years, and the lessons she taught me are ones I still carry in my heart. I was also lucky enough to work with a principal, Carol, who would pass on articles, books, or ideas to help me learn how to get my students excited about learning. Suzanne, who became my mentor, was another source of support and guidance during my learning process. These three individuals had a major impact on my teaching career.

A very special thanks goes to Dr. Lee Mountain, who offered endless support and encouragement throughout this long process. This book is actually the result of her prodding, pushing, coaxing, and nurturing. It is a joy and a privilege to have been her student and now to call her friend.

My appreciation also goes to the following reviewers for their comments on the manuscript: Sabrina Kotts, Athens City Schools; Cynthia Ferguson, Marbury School; and Beth Bayuk, Rutgers University. Last, I am extremely grateful for the guidance and support offered by Virginia Lanigan, Kris Lamarre, and Bridget Keane at Allyn and Bacon as well as Lynda Griffiths at TKM Productions.

1

Making the Connection

When I first began teaching, I found myself having to adapt rapidly to a framework for teaching that was more student centered than anything I had experienced. I began to take "baby steps" as I tried out the new ideas and techniques I had read so much about. Eventually, I began Atwell's (1987) reading workshop format with my students, where they self-selected the books they were reading. Periodically during the week, my students would also respond to what they had read in their response logs (Rief, 1992), and we would have mini-lessons on different strategies and techniques related to the reading process as discussed in Atwell (1987). In addition, I experimented with book projects in an attempt to strengthen reading-writing connections my students were incorporating into their literacy banks. These projects ranged from a variety of ways to respond to a book, including puppet theaters, designing book jackets, making mobiles, eight-page booklets, and time lines.

Although my students enjoyed the projects, I found that they began spending more and more time on the artistic aspects of the projects, and less and less time during the day reading, writing, and talking about their books with each other. It also seemed that even though the projects looked great, they never moved beyond a simple summarization of the literal elements of the story. This became a nagging concern, so I decided to continue reinforcing the reading-writing connection through mini-lessons, but instead of book projects after every book, I moved to asking students to do one book project every six to nine weeks. Sometimes we did the same projects together as a class, and other times the students chose the type of projects they would like to complete and share with the class. By changing to this format, we began to have ample time for reading books, responding in the logs, and meeting for weekly discussion groups and individual conference sessions.

As we became more comfortable with our reading workshop, our writing workshop began to evolve, too. In some cases, I found the students began to write stories reflecting the types of books they were reading in our reading workshop. This was most evident as we studied the critical elements of different genres in the books available in our classroom library. By the end of the year, it began to be difficult to differentiate between reading versus writing workshop. Instead of completing projects that encompassed only a basic retelling of the story, my students began critically analyzing, reflecting, and evaluating the complexities involved in reading and writing. They had questions about the author, how the author wrote, concepts of genre and mode, the reader's process, the reader's affect, the reader's own writing, and recommendations for reading (Atwell, 1987).

As I have followed these different literacy paths with my students, I have developed my own belief system toward language and literacy learning. These beliefs are based on my classroom experiences as a teacher and a student; my readings of professional educators and researchers; my participation in teacher study groups, district in-services, and workshops; and my being the mother of two young children embarking on their own literacy journeys. I have sat at my dining room table with Nancie Atwell, gone from the middle to the edge with Linda Rief, and made invitations and transitions with Regie Routman. Donald Graves helped with a fresh look at writing, along with lively discussions from Linda Gambrell and Janice Almasi. I have also learned from Carol Avery about the importance of a light touch, and, from Bobbi Fisher, how joyful learning can be. Along the way, Lev Vygotsky pointed out the importance of talk in children's learning, and how we educators must not isolate the social context in which it occurs.

Although these people do not know me, I feel as though I know them well. They are all very near and dear to my heart. They, along with others too numerous to mention, have been my advisors, confidantes, and friends as I have made my own literacy journey. Along with their insight and my experiences as a teacher, student, reader, and writer, I have had opportunities to expand my understandings, beliefs, attitudes, and practices regarding how I view teaching and learning, which I share with you:

▪ *Students must have opportunities to participate in meaningful activities that employ all aspects of language.* Listening, speaking, reading, and writing are utilized by students as they develop and extend their use of language to communicate and understand the world around them. Usually in combination, seldom in isolation, each process is embedded, to some extent, in the other.

This has become most evident in my 4-year-old daughter, Reghan. As a baby, when Reghan first became aware that she was being read to, she was more interested in getting control of the book and dropping it on the floor so she could watch Mommy or Daddy pick it up. Over time, she has moved from a basic reliance of simply viewing the pictures and listening to the story to speaking as she utilizes her knowledge of context and picture clues to help determine key parts of the story. She is now at the point of being somewhat familiar with the letters and sounds that make up the words in the pages of her book, so she often points out what she knows as we share books together.

This evolution in Reghan's development demonstrates how she has gradually moved from pointing out "Reghan's R" to using her knowledge of text to determine what some of the words might be. She has learned that the written text reflects the pictures, and that the letters on the page make up the words that help to tell the story. Reghan combines what she sees when she looks at the picture, the visual representation of the word, and the context she "hears" as the story is read aloud. This knowledge becomes tools to reinforce her skills and expertise as an emergent reader. The simple process of our sharing a book together helps connect and solidify her understandings of the connections that exist between the listening, speaking, and reading aspects of language to access the written language found within the pages of her book. By providing numerous opportunities such as this to interact with print in the classroom, we teachers reinforce, expand, and extend understanding of language for all the students with whom we work.

■ *Students have individual needs and developmental differences that I must respect, acknowledge, and nurture.* I have always felt it was somewhat unrealistic to expect the students who enter my classroom to all be at the same place in terms of their literacy skills. As their teacher, it is my job to learn everything I possibly can about what each student in my classroom already knows how to do. The child and I can then work together so that I can maximize and build toward the potential of each student. I expect no less of them, and I hope they expect no less of me.

One of my most exciting experiences was when I taught a multiage fourth/fifth-grade class with students who spoke English as a second language (ESL), students who had special needs, all the way to students who were gifted. There was no way that all of these students were going to know and be able to do the same kinds of things. By using a workshop format, I was able to individualize instruction according to the particular needs of each student. We would have small group mini-lessons targeting a particular convention or skill of reading and writing that only a few students might need. Other times, we would have large group mini-lessons that highlighted elements from which all the students would benefit. Sometimes I would give on-the-spot mini-lessons for a student during his or her individual conference sessions. In these sessions, I was able to gather probably the most valuable information I learned about my students. It was an opportunity for them to share their response logs, read portions of their book, or simply talk about the book and what they thought of it. It also was a way for them to share their thoughts, feelings, reservations, reflections, and even hyperventilations. In so doing, I was offered a window into their minds, hearts, and souls.

■ *Students should be actively involved in the planning and learning that occurs in the classroom.* At the beginning of the year, my multiage class and I sat down to brainstorm particular topics or themes we would like to cover for the year in science and social studies. Areas my students expressed an interest in included different wars, volcanoes, and skeletons. After further discussion, these themes were broadened into the larger themes of conflict, change, and structures. Together we would go to the library to select books for our classroom library, and together we thought of different projects we could do as a way of learning more about each different theme. The children's interest and motivation were most evident when these books and projects began to show up in our reading and writing workshop, too.

■ *Students respond to an environment that is conducive to social interaction and collaboration.* Many valuable insights can be gained by watching students who are encouraged to talk together, participate in problem solving, and negotiate and question each other. These include how they think, what they think, how they talk to each other, how they reason out their explanations, how they approach different situations and tasks, and how they respond to each other. One way to observe this is through the use of literature circles (also called literature study groups or book clubs) where students discuss the books they are reading together.

I had the opportunity to observe another teacher's group of fifth-grade students participating in literature study groups over the course of the school year. After the initial shock of not having to face me in our circle each week and retell what they read from start to finish, the students began to experiment with different ways of talking about the book. They explored the characters' motives, rethought what happened in the story based on looking at those actions from the characters' perspectives, and questioned the historical conditions surrounding certain story settings. At the end of the school year, each student was asked to share thoughts and reflections about his or her group experiences. It was impressive to note the sense of poise, self-esteem, and confidence the students displayed in their abilities to talk about the book together. They had experienced episodes of collaboration, interaction, as well as conflict, and, in their eyes, they were capable of dealing with all quite well.

▓ *Students look to each other and the teacher as a model and a guide.* I believe these elements I have mentioned throughout this discussion are embedded within each other, and the degree of overlap between each of them demonstrates the interconnection that exists. However, this last element is perhaps the most dominant thread. It is my job as a teacher to provide meaningful language opportunities that enable each student to maximize his or her own skills and abilities as a reader and writer. Critical to this is the fact that I must be certain there is ample time so that this may occur. Teachers and students should plan, talk, read, write, and listen to each other, since these are the voices that are a part of the community of learners. By doing so, we learn to respect and look to the members within our learning community for guidance and support. It is a way of working together to teach, model, and guide as we continually redefine new directions we take in our literacy journeys.

The Reading–Writing Connection

These particular elements of my belief system become guiding principles in how I invite my students to establish and reinforce connections that exist between reading and writing. After all, we are readers of what others have written, and we are writers of what we or others will read. However, students do not always recognize the connection between reading and writing. In many elementary schools, writing and reading are strangers to one another, isolated and taught as separate curriculum entities (Vacca, Vacca, & Gove, 1995). As teachers of students becoming readers and writers, it is important that we include reading and writing activities that enable our students to access what they know about both of these processes. Seven instructional principles proposed by Shanahan (1988) were based on his review of research concerning reading-writing relationships. He drew the following conclusions on how to combine reading and writing in the classroom to best enhance children's literacy learning:

1. *Teach both reading and writing.* Teachers need to provide as much reading and writing as possible, and both should be taught daily. Integration of reading and writing instruction can be useful, but only if children have reading and writing knowledge available for sharing.
2. *Introduce reading and writing from the earlier grades.* The use of the language experience approach (LEA) allows children to begin with oral composition and to use the teacher's transcriptions as a basis for learning about reading and writing. Encourage children to "pretend to write" or to "spell the words the way you think they should be spelled" is often all the impetus that is needed.
3. *Instruction should reflect the developmental nature of the reading-writing relationship.* At each reading level, teachers need to consider what the major goals of reading and writing instruction are for the children with whom they work. Instructional objectives then need to be examined for similar-

ities in content and purpose. Instruction and discussion should emphasize these similarities.

4. *Make the reading-writing connection explicit.* Do not assume that the transfer between the two is automatic. Instruction should encourage students to recognize the similarity of reading and writing, think about reading and writing relations, and reflect on how specific skills and information could be used in the other process.

5. *Instruction should emphasize content and process relations.* Product knowledge refers to facts, propositions, or principles; it can be substantive (e.g., knowledge of the world or of vocabulary) or structural (e.g., rules of syntax or organization plans). Both readers and writers require these types of information. Research on process relations indicate there is a sharing of thinking operations or problem-solving strategies across reading and writing. This pairing of processes or strategies that are analogous helps to emphasize the process relations that exist between reading and writing.

6. *Emphasize communication to make children more effective in negotiating social relations through written language.* The relationship that exists between reading and writing occurs between individuals, where reading and writing are communication processes, and texts are created by individuals in order to have an effect on others. Critical reading requires consideration of an author's intentions and an evaluation of the accuracy and quality of a text. Recognizing an author's purpose, attitude, tone, and mood is an important characteristic of reading comprehension. This can be accomplished through reading discussions that focus on authors and their purposes, as well as instruction in interpreting propaganda. Good writing reflects an awareness of knowledge and points of view likely to be represented in a potential audience. The writer then attempts to provide the reader with all necessary information in ways that will be effective.

7. *Teach reading and writing in meaningful contexts.* Provide a wide range of literacy experiences to ensure that children gain maximum benefit from reading-writing relations.

Although Shanahan's review of research emphasizes that reading and writing are not as alike as once supposed, there are other educational researchers and theorists who stress the commonalities to a greater degree (Applebee & Langer, 1984; Atwell, 1987; Tierney & Pearson, 1983; Vacca, Vacca, & Gove, 1995). Tierney and Pearson (1983) believe that in order to understand reading and writing connections, one must begin to view reading and writing as essentially similar processes of meaning construction. Both are acts of composing that include the following:

1. *Planning.* As a writer initially plans her writing, so a reader plans his reading.
2. *Drafting.* Drafting is defined as the refinement of meaning that occurs as readers and writers deal directly with the print on the page.
3. *Aligning.* Two facets of alignment are stances a reader or writer assumes in collaboration with his author or audience, and roles within which the reader or writer immerses himself as he proceeds with the topic.
4. *Revising.* If readers are to develop some control over and sense of discovery with the models of meaning they build, they must approach text with the same deliberation, time, and reflection that a writer employs as she revises a text.
5. *Monitoring.* Hand in hand with planning, aligning, drafting, and revising, readers and writers must be able to distance themselves from the texts they have created to evaluate what they have developed.

Tierney and Pearson (1983) view reading and writing as acts of composing involving continuous, recurring, and recursive transactions among readers and writers, their respective inner selves, and their perceptions of each other's goals and desires.

Atwell (1987) echoes this connection between reading and writing discussed by Tierney and Pearson. She, too, emphasizes this by discussing the similarities that exist in the rehearsing, drafting, and revising experienced by both readers and writers:

◼ Writers and readers *rehearse,* planning and predicting:
  — What will I write?
  — What will it be like?
  — How will it be shaped by my prior experiences as a writer?
  — What will I read?
  — What will it be like?
  — How will it be shaped by my prior experiences as a reader?
◼ Writers and readers *draft,* discovering meaning:
  — Where will these words I am writing take me?
  — Where will these words I am reading take me?
  — What surprises, disappointments, problems, questions, and insights will I encounter along the way?
◼ Writers and readers *revise,* reseeing and reseeking meaning:
  — Is this what I expected, what I hoped for?
  — What do I think of the words on the page?
  — What new thoughts do I think because of the words on the page?
  — What makes sense? What need to be changed so sense can be made?

Vacca, Vacca, and Gove (1995) underscore the strong bonds that exist between learning to write and learning to read. These connections are powerful enough to suggest that children probably learn as much about reading by writing as they learn about writing by reading. The authors point to a need to integrate reading and writing instruction, provide environments to support reading-writing connections, follow schedules that establish routines and procedures for writing, encourage response to texts through regular use of journals, and utilize children's literature and informational text to reinforce these reading and writing connections.

Relative to the types of reading and writing activities chosen by teachers, Applebee and Langer (1984) point to a need for teachers to judge the appropriateness of their instructional scaffolding by examining five aspects of language learning that were generalized from natural language-learning processes discussed by other researchers: intentionality, appropriateness, structure, collaboration, and internalization:

◼ To meet the criteria of *intentionality,* the task should have a clear overall purpose driving any separate activity that contributes to the whole. Eventual evaluation of students' success can be cast in terms of what they intended to accomplish.
◼ To meet the criteria of *appropriateness,* instructional tasks pose problems that can be solved with help but that students could not successfully complete on their own. These tasks should involve abilities that have not yet matured but are in the process of maturation.
◼ To meet the criteria of *structure,* modeling and questioning activities are structured around a model of appropriate approaches to the task and lead to a natural sequence of thought and language.
◼ To meet the criteria of *collaboration,* the teacher's response to student work recasts and expands on the students' efforts without rejecting what they have accomplished on their own.
◼ To meet the criteria of *internalization,* external scaffolding for the activity is gradually withdrawn as the patterns are internalized by the students.

In any area of the curriculum, this framework is generalizable to reading, writing, or discussion activities that integrate new learning with ways in which students express their knowledge, so that the processes of learning to read and write become intertwined in mutually supportive natural language activities (Applebee & Langer, 1984).

chapter **2**

Yes, but How Do I Do It?

Integral to the success of helping your students establish reading-writing connections is the importance of all aspects of language arts (e.g., listening, speaking, reading, and writing) in this process. Often, one aspect is that the focus area is so narrow that students fail to see that more than one area of language arts is usually present, or one is focused to such an extent that there is no opportunity for students to even think about using the other areas to mediate new ways of knowing and understanding.

Building Bridges

I like to think of the language arts as a way of building bridges between the different ways people understand and think. For example, my family enjoys comparing notes and thoughts on a particular book that one or more of us has read. The simple act of conversation as we talk about our reactions or the perplexities we experienced brings a different dimension to my thoughts about the book than I had experienced before we talked. In this instance, speaking through an informal book discussion served to help me understand aspects of the book that I had not understood before our conversation. Reading the book and talking about the book was a bridge that helped me travel further in how I understood it.

To expand further on the bridges or connections that exist between the different aspects of language, the following scenarios are similar to ones I have observed in my own classrooms. They provide an example of how students use these different aspects of listening, speaking, reading, and writing to monitor effectively their own literacy learning.

Three students are sitting in a corner of the classroom. One is reading aloud a draft of a paper she has written in writing workshop. She has decided she needs some feedback concerning the topic of her paper. She meets with the others in the conference area to read to them what she has written so far. The others listen attentively as the student reads from

respond to their own writing. It is a way to confer helpful responses to writers rather than critical attacks. As students become more adept at participating in this process, they will begin to try out alternative ways of approaching a problem, and they will listen to different perspectives offered by the group regarding a piece of writing in progress.

Avery (1993) discusses *roving conferences* as another way of providing opportunities for the teacher to demonstrate how to listen to a writer's story, followed by story confirmation through feedback, comments, and questions based on what was heard. In the roving conferences, Avery moves around the room as the writers are working, stopping periodically to consult with students. It is a way for her to listen to their struggles, ask questions, and possibly make suggestions, but it allows the writers to make their own decisions in working through the problem. Avery shares how the most demanding hours of teaching she has encountered have been when she was listening and responding to writers. Listening means hearing the words, reading the body language and voice tone, being aware of the child's behavior throughout the workshop, knowing the history of the current piece of writing and the child's process with this piece as well as past pieces, and connecting all this to the present moment.

Listening skills are essential if your students are to be successful in receiving, understanding, and responding to a message. Other activities in which students engage in listening include:

■ Read-alouds
■ Book tapes
■ Interviews
■ Literature discussion groups
■ Daily talks

SPEAKING

The most commonly used mode of expression is oral language. However, it is often not allowed as a means for the students to interact, debate, question, or mediate their learning. Since talk is a natural tool for students to use, it is important they be taught how to use speech effectively. The nature of talk in Atwell's writing workshop depends on what a writer needs or what he or she needs as a teacher of writers. Atwell shares that a whole range of different kinds of talk, suiting different purposes, goes on during a writing workshop. In conferencing sessions, dialogue occurs one-on-one between the teacher and student or between two students; other opportunities the students have to use speaking as a means of sharing language are in status-of-the class, where the whole class reports its plan for the day, group share, and writer's responses to their own writing (Atwell, 1987).

In Avery's class, she helped her first-grade children learn to talk about books by handling her role gingerly—sometimes offering her ideas, but quickly diminishing the importance of those ideas; accepting unconditionally the children's spontaneous thoughts; asking what they think and then welcoming those responses; striving to understand and delighting in their ideas; and, in the beginning, being cautious about expressing her own opinions. The delicate balancing act entailed in this process was most evident when a substitute teacher read a particular favorite book to the class, and the substitute's absolute answers annoyed the children to such a degree they did not want to read it again. For them, the magic came from considering possibilities; figuring out meaning from those possibilities; revising, refining, and clarifying that meaning; and doing it all through reading and rereading of the book in a community that talked and accepted a diversity of ideas (Avery, 1993).

Other activities where speaking is accentuated as an important communication skill and language process include:

■ Literature discussion circles
■ Sharing sessions
■ Shared reading
■ Storytelling
■ Reading aloud
■ Choral reading
■ Reader's theater
■ Paired reading
■ Reading or writing conference sessions

Of course, these are but a few suggestions. These activities become helpful in understanding the reciprocal relationship between speaking and listening. After all, when one speaks, it is usually with the thought that others are listening.

READING

Routman (1991) discusses the characteristics of a balanced reading program as including the following elements:

■ *Reading aloud* is the single-most influential factor in young children's success in learning to read. It improves listening skills, builds vocabulary, aids reading comprehension, and has a positive impact on students' attitudes toward reading.
■ *Shared reading*—in which a learner (or group of learners) sees the text, observes an expert (usually the teacher) reading it with fluency and expression, and is invited to read along—is a rewarding experience. The learner is in the role of receiving support, and the teacher-expert accepts and encourages all efforts and approximations the learner (the novice) makes.
■ *Guided reading* is the heart of the instructional reading program. Here, the teacher meets with students to think critically about the book. Group time is spent in discussion, in appreciating and enjoying the language of literature, and in sharing personal and group insights. Formats range from whole-class, small-group, or individualized guided reading.
■ *Independent reading,* the opportunity for students to read self-selected books, is an indispensable part of a balanced reading program. Students are in charge of their own reading—by choosing their own books, doing their own reading, and taking responsibility to work through the challenges of the text. Time must be provided in school for students to read the books of their choice. Teachers have found that independent reading works well by beginning with 5 to 10 minutes a day and working up to 30 minutes or more daily of SSR (sustained silent reading), RR (recreational reading), DIRT (daily independent reading time), DEAR (drop everything and read), or whatever the teacher chooses to call this time. In some cases, independent reading may be the mainstay of the reading program.

When students have daily opportunities to interact with books, they absorb information relating to conventions of writing, story schema, story structure, relationships between story elements, vocabulary, and point of view, and they can participate in story retelling. In addition, students develop the ability to plan, check, monitor, revise, and evaluate their unfolding comprehension (Reutzel & Cooter, 1996). Evidence of student success in classrooms and programs that encourage and support multiple opportunities to interact with text include those of Nancie Atwell (1987), Linda Rief (1992), Regie Routman (1991), Carol Avery (1993), and Bobbie Fisher (1991).

The types of knowledge students acquire range the gamut from the most literal to reflective critical thinking opportunities, usually dependent on the type of stance the children adopt during the reading event. Falling somewhere within an efferent-aesthetic continuum, a particular stance determines the degree to which the public (tip of the iceberg) or private (base of the iceberg) elements will fall within the range of a reader's attention (Rosenblatt, 1994). The efferent stance focuses on the cognitive, the referential, the factual, the analytic; the aesthetic stance pays more attention to the sensuous, the affective, the emotive, and the qualitative (Rosenblatt, 1994). In most reading situations, usually one stance is more predominant over the other, and its selection is one of the earliest and most important steps in the reading event. This stance taken by the reader is a major factor in the types of information the reader takes away from the reading experience.

Other activities in which students participate in reading include literature discussion groups, DRTA (Directed Reading and Thinking Activity), SQ3R (Survey, Question, Read, Recite, and Review), story retellings, and reader's theater.

WRITING

> In order to read like a writer we engage with the author in what the author is writing, and we anticipate what the author will say, so that the author is in effect writing on our behalf, not showing how something is done but doing it with us. . . . Bit by bit, one thing at a time, but enormous things over the passage of time, the learner learns through reading like a writer to write like a writer. (Smith, 1983)

Writing is a way for students to understand what they are thinking. They need daily opportunities to participate in writing activities in which they will be successful. Tompkins (1998) discusses class collaboration as a way of introducing the writing process. The teacher acts as a guide, modeling the process he or she moves through as an author, and students are able to practice the process approach to writing in a supportive environment. Tompkins states that these "group compositions" can serve as a dry run during which students' questions and misconceptions can be clarified. As students participate in their own writing projects, mini-lessons provide further opportunities for the students to learn how to move through the five stages of the writing process, how to gather and organize ideas for writing, how to participate in writing groups, how to proofread, and how to share their writing (Tompkins, 1998).

Findings from two teacher-researchers also emphasize the importance of students experiencing a sense of authorship:

- In Bobbi Fisher's (1991) kindergarten class, her children write daily for a variety of purposes, so the process of writing is part of the everyday routine in her classroom. She found that by doing this, her children began to think of themselves as writers and became engaged in the writing process for their own needs and interests.
- Nancie Atwell (1987) states that when students have regular, frequent time set aside to write, writing can play a crucial role in helping them to grow up, making it possible for them to capture who they are and then come back and measure themselves against that earlier self. She emphasizes that setting aside a regular time for writing that the students can always count on allows them some control over this distance between their past and present.

Writing is a time for stories to be read, books to be published, poems to be recited, plays to be acted, songs to be sung, newspapers to be shared, letters to be mailed, jokes to be told, notes to be passed, cards to be sent, cartons to be labeled, instructions to be followed, designs to be made, recipes to be cooked, messages to be exchanged, programs to be organized, excursions to be planned, catalogs to be compared, entertainment guides to be consulted, memos to be circulated, announcements to be posted, bills to be collected, posters to be displayed, cribs to be hidden, and diaries to be concealed (Smith, 1983). Writing can be used to consolidate students' thinking about texts by using such instructional strategies as writing summaries, devising story alternatives, completing a K-W-L chart (What I Know, What I Want to Know, and What I Learned), and organizing webs (Barr & Johnson, 1997). Writing can be integrated with reading to expand students' thinking about text through the use of dialectic journals, letter writing, text pattern writing, persuasive writing, quick writes, and directed reading-writing lessons (Barr & Johnson, 1997).

Most important however, writing is for ideas, action, reflection, and experience; it is not for having one's ignorance exposed, one's sensitivity destroyed, or one's ability assessed (Smith, 1983). The knowledge that writers require is in existing texts, and it is there for the reading (Smith, 1983).

VIEWING

Viewing refers to the need for students to be able to comprehend a broad range of visual media, including films, videos, plays, television, bulletin board/displays, photographs, book illustrations, advertisements, visits to the museum, computer graphics in instructional software, and CD-ROMs. Tompkins (1998) emphasizes that students need to integrate visual knowledge with other literacy knowledge. Key concepts she discusses concerning viewing include:

- Viewing is an important component of literacy.
- Students view visual media for a variety of purposes.
- Viewing is much like reading, and students use comprehension strategies in both reading and viewing.
- Students use story boards to examine the illustrations in books.
- Students learn about propaganda techniques in order to critically analyze commercials and advertisements.

Viewing as an element of the language arts is extremely relevant to the world your students live in today. They are constantly surrounded by a mass of graphics, images, and information, and they need to be able to access that information. They also need to know how to communicate and share the information, which leads naturally into the visual representation element of the language arts.

VISUALLY REPRESENTING

A sign is something that represents an object, a set of objects, or a phenomenon—it is a symbol with a specific meaning that has evolved in the history of a culture (Dixon-Krauss, 1996). Our culture has created a sign system that serves to foster communication and thinking. These sign systems can include numbers, graphics, written text, dialogue/talk, art, music, and body language/movement. Through the process of visually representing, students utilize these sign systems to create meaning. This semiotic mediation enables them to move from lower forms of mental behavior to higher, cultural forms of behavior. Tompkins (1998) discusses video productions, hypertext and other computer programs, story quilts, and illustrations on charts, posters, and books students are writing as examples of multiple sign systems used to facilitate meaning making.

Focusing on a Genre

One way to study literature is through a focus on genres, or types of literature. Tompkins and Hoskisson (1991) recommend an instructional strategy to teach children about a genre that then can be used to help children read:

1. Review information about literature to determine unique characteristics or features.
2. Collect a text set representative of a genre, then preview the books to further examine characteristics or features (prior to setting them out for students to read).
3. Prepare questions to focus children's attention on distinguishing characteristics and prepare a descriptive chart that lists these characteristics.
4. Share literature that clearly provides examples of the genre, ask focusing questions pertinent to the characteristics, and introduce the chart as a way of summarizing the discussion.
5. Repeat the steps with another selection, and discuss how it exemplifies the same characteristics of the genre.
6. Provide extending activities to extend the students' knowledge of the genre through further reading, retelling, dramatizing, or writing activities.

Chapters 3, 4, and 5 of this book follow these guidelines to a certain extent. The characteristics of the genres included are introduced in the first part of the chapter, then activities that are representative of the characteristics are delineated with suggestions and guidelines for teaching. Following the reading activities, a sample writing activity is included that encourages the students to think more globally as they synthesize information they learned in order to write a story in that particular genre. The last section of each chapter includes technology projects that teachers and students may decide to utilize in connection with their study of each genre, as well as an annotated bibliography and supplementary materials helpful in addressing each genre.

INTRODUCTION OF THE GENRE

Information about each genre is included to serve as a reference point when introducing it to the class. The definition, interesting information, and genre characteristics are included. Discussion of each characteristic is followed by summaries of books that serve to highlight the characteristic. Genres discussed in this book include:

▨ Folktales
▨ Fables
▨ Legends

These three genres are part of the broader category of folk literature.

WHAT IS FOLK LITERATURE?

Folk literature, sometimes called *folklore* or *mythology* (Huck, Hepler, & Hickman, 1987), refers to all of the stories that have been created as a result of the oral tradition. These creations were a way for people to explain the world to their primitive minds. Folk literature expresses people's interpretation of the relationships among human beings and their fears and desires; it records the mores and the cultural patterns of the society from which it stems; and it gives expressions to such deep universal emotions as joy, grief, fear, jealousy, and awe (Sutherland, 1997). The storytellers told these tales again and again around the fires of the early tribes, by the hearths of humble cottages, in front of the great fire in the king's hall; they told them as they sat in the grass huts of the jungle, the hogans of the Navajo, and the igloos of the Eskimo (Huck, Hepler, & Hickman, 1987). Games, songs, nursery rhymes, verses, proverbs, folktales, fables, myths, legends, and epics were passed down across many generations to reflect the accumulated wisdom and memory of people.

IMPORTANCE AND VALUE OF FOLK LITERATURE

This traditional literature derived from human imagination to explain the human condition forms the foundation of understandings of life as expressed in modern literature (Huck, Hepler, & Hickman, 1987), and it is the foundation upon which all children's literature is based (Abrahamson, 1995). Children respond to the stories from folk literature associated with children's literature for many reasons (Huck, Hepler, & Hickman, 1987):

- The stories are good, short, and have fast-moving plots.
- They are frequently humorous and almost always end happily.
- Poetic justice prevails; the good and the just are eventually rewarded, while the evil are punished.
- Wishes come true after the fulfillment of a task or trial.
- The smallest child, youngest son, and smallest animal usually succeed, while the oldest or largest is frequently defeated.
- Folktales kindle the child's imagination.

By reading folk literature from other cultures, children are offered opportunities to extend the meaning of language, and they are provided insights into the beliefs of these people, their values, their jokes, their life-styles, and their histories (Huck, Hepler, & Hickman, 1987). It becomes a way that the reader can enter into another culture and recognize the universality of the wishes, dreams, and problems of people around the world (Bosma, 1987). The types of folk literature included within this book are helpful in providing students the opportunities to explore, reflect, and extend their own imaginations, as they seek to understand and deal with the world around them.

ACTIVITIES REPRESENTATIVE OF EACH GENRE'S CHARACTERISTICS

In Chapters 3, 4, and 5, this section takes the characteristics discussed in the first part of the chapter and provides focus activities that can be used as guidelines when teaching. Each focus activity reviews the characteristic, activity, summary, and materials. The rest of the lesson is in a procedural format that includes examples, guidelines, and suggestions that may be utilized for instruction. Examples of activities that are included are:

- Plot graphs that represent an analysis of rising action, climax, and falling action
- Character analysis charts or shields to assist to determining pertinent information about the character
- Mobiles that emphasize the repetitive patterns found within the genre
- Comic strips to illustrate key story elements

■ Maps to analyze settings, actions, and key events
■ Puppet theaters to use in story analysis and retelling
■ Cause/effect graphics to illustrate conflict relationships
■ Time lines to illustrate sequencing of events
■ Maps to analyze attitudes and values representative of a culture.

In addition, lesson extensions are offered as a means of extending and connecting information the students are absorbing. Time frame guidelines are also included.

CONNECTING THE WRITING PROCESS WITH THE GENRE

Students expand their knowledge of a story through writing, and they can expand their knowledge about a literary genre by writing stories that embody the characteristics of a genre they have studied (Tompkins, 1990). Students use their prior literature experiences to serve as prewriting, and these extensive reading activities help to make the writing successful (Tompkins & McGee, 1993). Activities included in this book that highlight the connection between reading and writing include:

■ Story transformations that change aspects of story elements to rewrite the story
■ Writing and illustrating original comic strips
■ Publishing a class newspaper

At the beginning of this section of Chapters 3, 4, and 5, a chart summarizes the stage of writing that is highlighted and the activity that illustrates it. The lesson is then presented in a format that corresponds to the stages of the writing process (see Figure 2.1). It is important to emphasize that the stages of the

FIGURE 2.1 Recursive Stages of the Writing Process

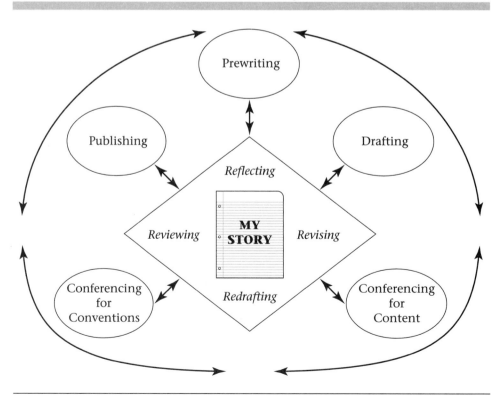

writing process are extremely recursive, thus, a writer may often revisit a previous stage in order to start over, further develop the draft, or seek assistance or guidance from a peer or teacher. Suggestions for mini-lessons related to the writing process are also included.

The importance of scheduling daily time for students to write, so that they have opportunities to move through the writing process, has been chronicled with students in kindergarten through junior high school by Atwell (1987), Rief (1992), Routman (1991), Avery (1993), and Fisher (1991). The stages of the writing process that are followed in this book include prewriting, drafting, conferencing for content, conferencing for conventions, and publishing:

PREWRITING

- Select a topic for writing.
- Decide on an audience.
- Determine who will tell the story (point of view).
- Decide how to organize ideas for writing.
- Use what the writer knows to help in writing.
- Gather other materials necessary that will serve as a resource when writing.

DRAFTING

- Get ideas down on paper.
- Leave space for revisions.
- Use what the writer knows and other materials gathered as an aid.
- Reread the draft while writing.
- Look back at what other authors have done in their books (beginning the story, introducing the setting, presenting the problem, using dialogue, weaving the character's nature into the story, building events, resolving the problem, making conclusions).

CONFERENCING FOR CONTENT

- Talk with others when the writer gets "stuck."
- Readers look for holes in what has been written.
- Readers ask the question, "Does it make sense?"
- Discuss the draft with a peer or peers.
- Talk with the teacher about the draft.

CONFERENCING FOR CONVENTIONS OF WRITING

- Focus on capitalization, usage, punctuation, and spelling.
- Participate in an editing conference with a peer.
- Participate in an editing conference with the teacher.

PUBLISHING

- Decide how to publish the piece (e.g., picture book, chapter book, article, letter).
- Share the finished piece with others.
- Send the piece off for publication.

Embedded within the entire process is the notion that the students move through a cycle of reflecting, revising, redrafting, and reviewing:

REFLECTING

- Asking yourself, "Does it make sense?"

▥ What can be added to help make the story better?
▥ Place questions marks by places in the text that need more work.

REVISING

▥ Use some of what others have suggested for content to help improve the draft.
▥ Substitute, delete, or move places in the draft when necessary.
▥ Fill in any holes that make the ideas in the text unclear.

REDRAFTING

▥ Do you want to start over on a new story?
▥ Do you want to take one aspect of the current story and use it to write a new draft?

REVIEWING

▥ Determine if the flow of the piece works.
▥ Self-check to look at capitalization, usage, punctuation, and spelling before moving on to a teacher or peer-editing conference.
▥ Do a final check for content and conventions before moving on to publication.

As each stage of the writing process is introduced in Chapters 3, 4, and 5, a chart is included that highlights the key activities that are useful in guiding the students. Mini-lessons are included periodically throughout the writing lesson to provide suggestions regarding strategies and techniques that need to be modeled by the teacher so that students are comfortable with new ideas and concepts.

CONNECTING READING AND WRITING

Readers and writers use similar strategies as they interact with print to construct meaning. Therefore, it is important that we help them see, hear, and experience these relationships. Classroom connections that can be utilized as a means of helping establish this relationship include (Tompkins, 1998):

▥ Help writers assume alternative points of view as potential readers.
▥ Help readers consider the writer's purpose and viewpoint.
▥ Point out that reading is much like composing, so that students will view reading as a process, much like the writing process.
▥ Talk with students about the similarities between the reading and writing processes.
▥ Talk with students about reading and writing strategies.

The use of journals is also helpful in making the connection between reading and writing. Dialogue journals involve a written conversation between the teacher and student about any topic of interest. The use of buddy journals involves a written conversation between pairs of children. They can write about books that were read or any other topic of interest. They tend to be highly motivating, and serve a functional, meaningful role in connecting reading and writing, because children love to read what other children have written (Vacca, Vacca, & Gove, 1995). An alternative format is that of reading logs, which offer a more structure response to books that are read. In this type of journal, the teacher usually provides a prompt to guide students' writing after reading a text.

One other type of journal is the literature response log, where readers are invited to respond freely to text without being prompted (Vacca, Vacca, &

Gove, 1995). The students are encouraged to relate the book to their own experiences, ask questions to help make sense of the text, make predictions as the plot unfolds, and change their predictions as they precede through the text. Other ways to respond to the book include:

- ▪ "Talk" to the characters as a way of offering advice or approving/disapproving of their values, actions, or behaviors.
- ▪ Praise or criticize the book, the author, or the literary style.

In general, the literature response journal is a way to record those fleeting thoughts that pass through the students' minds as they interact with the book (Vacca, Vacca, & Gove, 1995). They should be encouraged to keep the journals close to their sides as they read, so that they can write and respond whenever a thought strikes.

SHIFTING CONTROL AND RESPONSIBILITY

A major premise of this book is to encourage students to gradually take control of their reading and writing as well as to emphasize the social nature of learning as a tool in literacy development. Through effective teacher modeling and guidance, students will acquire new strategies and skills with which to monitor their literacy processes. It is also important to remember that students work at different rates and levels of understandings, and by accommodating these individual needs in the classroom with a flexible schedule that provides time and opportunity to read and write, your students will be much more successful in their experiences. The use of literature as a springboard to connect to writing serves to reinforce developing processes in reading and writing within each individual student.

The activities included illustrate the possibilities and directions that can be taken in helping students learn about a particular genre, but they are not restricted to the one particular genre to which they have been included. These activities can be taken and easily adapted to other genres that may be studied during the year. It is also important to emphasize continuously the connections between reading and writing so that your students will recognize and utilize their knowledge of these relationships to further develop their own literacy.

chapter **3**

All about Folktales

What Is a Folktale?

Folktales are magical stories of unknown authorship that have been passed down orally from generation to generation. Eventually, the oral versions of the story were written down. Types of stories discussed within this genre include cumulative tales, talking beast tales, and wonder tales.

Is There Only One Version of a Folktale?

There are many different variants of the same folktale that are dependent, in large part, on the country in which they originate. For example, *Lon Po Po* by Ed Young is a "Little Red Riding Hood" story from China, and *Petrosinella* by Diane Stanley is the story of a Neapolitan "Rapunzel." A variant has basically the story or plot as the original, but it may have different characters, a different setting, and perhaps different motifs (Huck, Hepler, & Hickman, 1987). *Yeh-Shen* and *Vasilisa the Beautiful* are both different versions of "Cinderella." In *Yeh-Shen,* the magic fish bestows gifts upon the girl, whereas in *Vasilisa the Beautiful,* it is the doll made for her by her mother. Other stories that have many different variations include "The Three Little Pigs," "The Gingerbread Boy," and "Jack and the Beanstalk" (Tompkins & McGee, 1993). Children may compare these different variants by using classroom-made charts, with the tale titles going down the left margin and these topics listed across the top (Huck, Hepler, & Hickman, 1987):

- Opening and ending conversations
- Origin of the tale
- Clues to the country of origin
- Talents of the characters

- Tasks to be done
- Verses, refrains, chants, and their outcomes
- Illustrations
- Special or unique vocabulary

By studying the different variants of a folktale, the students can enjoy exploring differences and similarities in theme and motif represented across cultures.

Types of Folktales

There are various groups into which folktales can be categorized. Three of the most well-known include cumulative tales, talking beast tales, and wonder tales (or fairy tales):

1. Cumulative tales build around the repetition of words and events. The charm of a cumulative tale lies in its minimum plot and maximum rhythm. Its episodes follow each other neatly and logically in a pattern of cadenced repetition (Sutherland, 1997). Examples are:
   - "Henny Penny"
   - "The Gingerbread Boy"
   - "The House That Jack Built"
2. Talking beast tales are stories where the animals talk and act like humans. These beast tales generally teach a lesson—usually the folly of credulity and the rewards of courage, ingenuity, and independence—though their didacticism (lesson that is taught) does not stand out as much as it does in fables (Sutherland, 1997). Examples are:
   - "The Three Little Pigs"
   - "Puss 'n' Boots"
3. Wonder tales, or fairy tales, include fantastic characters such as witches, giants, and fairy godmothers (Tompkins & McGee, 1993). The witches and wizards are usually wicked, and they cast spells that turn noble youths into beasts (Sutherland, 1997). The bad giants must be dealt with using deceit and trickery, and usually they are thickheaded, so that clever boys and girls can easily befuddle them. The good giants are often helpful to the characters in the story, giving aid only to honest folk who shine in the grace of goodness (Sutherland, 1997). In some, fairy godmothers aid the major character of the story in some way. Examples are:
   - "Snow White"
   - "Sleeping Beauty"

What Are the Characteristics of Folktales?

Characteristics that folktales have in common include:

- A simple storyline resulting in a satisfying conclusion
- A strong sense of magic
- A clear-cut characterization
- The use of repetition in the narrative

Although all of these characteristics may be found within a folktale, all do not have to be present to categorize it as belonging to that genre. For the most part, if several of these characteristics are represented, along with the presence of motifs, then it is safe to consider the story a folktale.

Motifs

The presences of motifs, or small recurring elements, is also helpful in identifying stories that are folktales. Motifs have been defined as the smallest part of a tale that can exist independently (Huck, Hepler, & Hickman, 1987). Every folktale has at least a few of these motifs; some of the more common ones are (Huck, Hepler, & Hickman, 1987; Tompkins & McGee, 1993):

- A long sleep or enchantment (e.g., "Snow White")
- The use of magical powers (e.g., "The Fisherman and His Wife")
- Magical transformations (e.g., "Beauty and the Beast")
- The presence of magical objects (e.g., "Vasilisa the Beautiful")
- The granting of wishes (e.g., "The Seven Ravens")
- The use of trickery (e.g., "Puss 'n' Boots")

There are other motifs that may be found within the story. In some cases, these motifs can be seen in the recurring parade of characters in folktales—such as the younger brother, the wicked stepmother, the abused child, or the clever trickster (Huck, Hepler, & Hickman, 1987). As the study of folktales progresses, the class can compile a list of different motifs found while reading the stories.

Summary

The most popular types of stories that represent the genre of folktales include cumulative tales, talking beast tales, and fairy tales. Characteristics of folktales that are helpful in identifying stories to represent this genre include a simple storyline with a satisfying conclusion, a strong sense of magic, clear-cut characterization, the triumph of good over evil, and the use of repetition in the narrative. In addition, every folktale has small, recurring elements called motifs, which are helpful when analyzing the story.

Reading Folktales: What Are Examples of Each Characteristic from Actual Folktales?

In this section, each characteristic will be discussed, books will be given to illustrate the characteristic, and a sample lesson idea is presented as a means of expanding students' knowledge and comprehension of the story.

CHARACTERISTIC: A SIMPLE STORYLINE RESULTING IN A SATISFYING CONCLUSION

The story often begins with "Once upon a time" and ends with "And they lived happily ever after." The parts of the story in between involve moving from one event to the next in fairly rapid succession. In addition, the setting is so generalized that it could be located anywhere.

In *The Sleeping Beauty,* retold and illustrated by Trina Schart Hyman, the king throws a birthday celebration for his newborn daughter. His discourtesy to the uninvited thirteenth fairy results in a curse on the king's daughter, which is lightened somewhat by the gift of another fairy. The curse is broken after 100 years by the kiss of a prince.

> *Summary:* Disgruntled fairy casts curse on beautiful princess. The spell is later broken by kiss of devoted prince.

In *Petrosinella,* retold and illustrated by Diane Stanley, a mother's love is not enough to keep an Ogress from taking the woman's daughter. Petrosinella is taken deep into a forest and placed in a tower high above the trees. The Ogress visits Petrosinella by climbing the girl's hair like a ladder. A prince happens by and falls in love with Petrosinella. He and Petrosinella together outwit the Ogress. Petrosinella is reunited with her mother at her marriage to the prince.

> *Summary:* Wicked old woman imprisons beautiful young girl. A prince passing by falls in love with her, and, together, they outwit the wicked old woman.

Rumpelstiltskin, retold and illustrated by Paul O. Zelinsky, is based on the Brothers Grimm earliest versions of the story. The miller's daughter is forced to spin three rooms full of straw into gold, or she will lose her life. A tiny man helps her each night in exchange for, first, her necklace, then her ring, and finally her first child born when she is queen. The king marries the miller's daughter, she bears a child, and the little man returns to collect on the queen's promise. Moved by her tears, he gives her three days to guess his name. At the last possible moment, the queen learns the little man's name, thus saving her newborn daughter.

> *Summary:* Woman saved from death by magic of little man. Little man returns for her daughter. Mother learns little man's name and saves daughter.

FOCUS ACTIVITY: A SIMPLE STORYLINE

■ Characteristic: A simple storyline resulting in a satisfying conclusion
■ Activity: Plot graph
■ Summary: The plot graph will be used to represent the rising action, climax, and falling action found within the fairy tale.
■ Materials: Folktales, Reproducible 3.1 (Story Events for Plot Graph), Reproducible 3.2 (Plot Graph with Key)

How Do You Do It?

Select a fairy tale to read with the class. Instruct the students to listen for the major events in the story. After the story is read, discuss with the students what are the most important events. List the events in chronological order on the board (or on Reproducible 3.1)—for example:

1. The queen forces Snow White to work in the kitchen from dawn to dusk.
2. The Magic Mirror tells the queen that Snow White is the fairest maiden in the land.
3. The queen orders the woodcutter to take Snow White to the woods and kill her. The woodcutter tells Snow White to run away and don't come back.
4. Snow White flees into the woods and comes across the little house where the Seven Dwarfs live. Snow White decides to live with the Seven Dwarfs and take care of them.
5. The queen discovers from the Magic Mirror that Snow White is still alive. The queen turns herself into a witch and takes Snow White a poison apple.
6. Snow White takes a bite of the poison apple and falls into a deep sleep.
7. The Seven Dwarfs chase the evil queen away. The evil queen falls to her death off the mountain.

8. The Seven Dwarfs place Snow White in a glass coffin and watch over her day and night.
9. A prince riding by on his horse falls in love with Snow White. He kisses Snow White and wakes her up from the sleep.
10. The prince takes Snow White to his castle where they live happily ever after.

Using chart paper, chalkboard, or overhead, draw a horizontal and vertical axis (see Figure 3.1 and Reproducible 3.2). The vertical axis is used to rate the events in terms of calm to exciting. The horizontal axis represents the most important events discussed in the first part of the activity (items 1–10). As a class, complete the plot graph together. Let the students discuss with a partner where the events should be rated, then come to a class consensus.

After plotting all of the events, select which event was the most exciting and which event was the least exciting. Students can create a key out to the side of or below the graph to represent this. Figure 3.2 shows the key and a sample completed graph. Other ways to analyze the story are to look at good and evil, happy and sad, or positive and negative.

Next, let students read their own fairy tale. This can be done as a small group activity (3 or 4 students), in partners, or individually. After the story is read, tell students to come up with 7 to 10 events that are most important to the story. They follow this by plotting their graph. After everyone is done, each group provides summaries for the stories by sharing their plot graph. The groups should also identify on their plot graphs the least and most exciting events in the story.

Extensions

1. The students can also illustrate their graphs with pictures that represent each event. Each group's graph with key, events, and pictures can then be used to create individual pages in a class book.
2. This activity transforms easily into a bulletin board of the students' work. Students write the title of the story and numbered events on index cards. These are placed out to the side of the graph.

Note: This activity can be broken into a two-day lesson:

Day One would consist of the class analyzing a fairy tale together, and then together plotting a graph with discussion of ways to evaluate (least exciting/ most exciting) the story.

FIGURE 3.1 Graph for Plotting Key Events of the Story

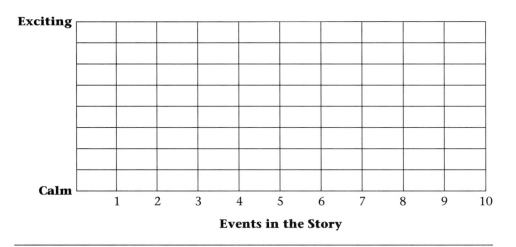

FIGURE 3.2   Graph for Plotting Key Events of the Story with Sample Key for Least Exiting and Most Exiting Events

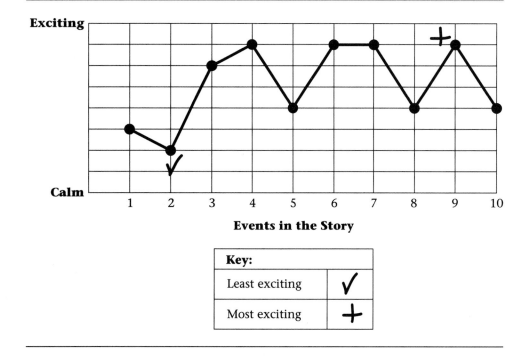

Events in the Story

Key:	
Least exciting	✓
Most exciting	+

Day Two follows with the class working in small groups, partners, or as individuals to analyze their own folktales and plot the graph.

Reproducible masters 3.1 and 3.2 may be found at the end of this chapter.

CHARACTERISTIC: A STRONG SENSE OF MAGIC

This characteristic may be represented by characters who have magical powers, actual transformations by the characters from one form to another, or the presence of magical objects.

Marianna Mayer retells the classic Russian story of *Baba Yaga and Vasilisa the Brave.* Beautiful Vasilisa lives with her jealous stepmother and stepsisters in a house on the edge of a dark forest. Her only companion and friend is a doll (that comes alive) made by her mother before she died. Her stepmother sends her off to Baba Yaga, a witch, to bring back a candle to light their home. Taking her doll with her, Vasilisa leaves on the errand from which she has little hope of returning alive. Baba Yaga takes Vasilisa into her house, and the little doll labors tirelessly to complete the tasks Baba Yaga leaves for Vasilisa. At last, Baba Yaga sends Vasilisa home with a lighted skull from her fencepost. The skull turns Vasilisa's stepmother and stepsisters into flames, and Vasilisa is taken in by an elderly woman with no children. Vasilisa shows her gratitude to the woman by spinning thread so light and delicate that the old woman takes it as a gift to the tzar's palace. The tzar falls in love with Vasilisa and takes her as his wife.

Summary: The magic of Vasilisa's doll helps her outwit her wicked stepmother and Baba Yaga.

Jack and the Beanstalk, retold and illustrated by John Howe, once again finds lazy Jack trading his cow for five brightly colored magic beans. After his mother throws the beans out the window in disgust at his stupidity, the beanstalk grows high into the sky over night. Jack climbs the beanstalk three times, taking the giant's hen that lays golden eggs, his bag of gold, and his singing harp. The giant pursues Jack, and Jack cuts down the beanstalk, whereupon the giant tumbles to his death.

> *Summary:* Jack climbs the beanstalk that grew after his mother threw the beans out the window. He visits the giant's kingdom and takes the giant's hen that lays golden eggs, bag of gold, and singing harp.

Another classic tale by the Brothers Grimm is *The Seven Ravens,* adapted by Laura Geringer with paintings by Edward S. Gazsi. In this version, a young girl finds seven dusty boxes under her parents' bed that contains seven shirts. Her parents break down into tears, and tell her the story of her brothers turned into ravens after her father cried out at them in rage. The girl leaves on a journey to find her brothers, taking with her only a loaf of bread, a jug of water, and a wooden stool. Over her own shirt, she wears her brothers' shirts that had been made by their mother with patterns of the sun, the moon, and the stars woven into them. After encounters with the sun, the moon, and the stars, her quest takes her to the Glass Mountain, where she finds the seven ravens. When the brothers slip on the shirts made by their mother, they turn back into little boys. The eldest brother, still a raven, flies them home, and he then slips on his rainbow shirt and turns back into a little boy.

> *Summary:* A young girl journeys to find her brothers who were turned into ravens. After encounters with the sun, the moon, and the stars, the girl arrives at the Glass Mountain, where she is reunited with her seven brothers. The shirts made by their mother helps return them to their human form.

FOCUS ACTIVITY: A STRONG SENSE OF MAGIC

- ■ Characteristic: A strong sense of magic
- ■ Activity: Fantasy/reality chart
- ■ Summary: The fantasy/reality chart will be used to analyze magical events in the story. This is then countered by the students identifying why the elements are fiction.
- ■ Materials: Figure 3.3 (Fantasy/Reality Chart), Reproducible 3.3 (Magic Scavenger Hunt)

How Do You Do It?

Discuss with the students what is meant by the words *fantasy* and *reality.* Brainstorm the types of things that could be present in a story that would identify them as fantasy or reality. Some examples include:

1. Beans can grow in Jack's yard (reality), but magic beans would not grow into a vine that reaches into the giant's kingdom (fantasy).
2. Chickens do lay eggs (reality), but the eggs are not made of pure gold (fantasy).

After reading *The Seven Ravens,* discuss with the students which events in the story were fantasy and which were based on reality (see Figure 3.3). Another column could be added on the right so that the class may write in a brief statement as to why the event is either fantasy or reality.

The discussion of which events in the story are fantasy or reality can easily be accomplished in a informal discussion setting. Encourage the students to discuss what it is that makes each of the events either fantasy or reality. Students also enjoy analyzing piece by piece to explicitly identifying what could have happened and what could not have happened—for instance:

> *It is possible for the father to have been very angry at the brothers for waking up the girl when she was a baby, but it is not possible for his anger to have turned the boys into ravens.*

FIGURE 3.3 Fantasy/Reality Chart

EVENT	FANTASY OR REALITY
The young girl found the seven dusty boxes containing shirts her mother had made for her brothers underneath the bed.	Reality
Her father tells the story of her seven brothers being turned into ravens.	Fantasy
The girl sets out on a journey to find her brothers.	Reality

Once the students have analyzed the story together, they can easily identify parts of stories they are reading (either as part of a literature discussion group or an individualized reading program) that are fantasy or reality. It is not necessary to analyze the whole story every time. The students can easily identify one or two major events in their story as either fantasy or reality.

To broaden the students' understanding of fantasy/reality, have a scavenger hunt where the students locate characters, events, or objects associated with magic from all the different folktales they have read (see Figure 3.4 and Reproducible 3.3).

If the study of folktales has just begun, then this could be an ongoing activity. Different groups of students could decide what to "find" and add to the list each week. The students' findings across the different folktales could be organized into a larger class tracking chart of "magic" found within the books. This is easily tied back into the motifs often represented in folktales. Possible headings could include Magical Objects, Transformations, and Magical Powers. The students can add their own categories as they come across other motifs related to magic. Relate these discussions back to the differentiation between fantasy and reality.

Extensions
1. As part of a journal activity, the students can write from the perspective of another character in the story—for instance: "Caaaw, caaaw, what is happening to me? Where am I? Why am I covered in black feathers?"
2. For younger students: After the students have identified one or two events that are fantasy/reality in their own stories they are reading, ask them to write the events on separate index cards with the event on one side and the answer on the other. Make a simple gameboard out of poster or tag

FIGURE 3.4 Sample Form for Students to Record Items Found in the Scavenger Hunt

WHAT DID YOU FIND?	EXAMPLE	WHERE DID YOU FIND IT?
An object used to protect the character	Her brothers' shirts protect a young girl as she searches for them.	*The Seven Ravens*
A character who changes form	Snow White's stepmother changes into an old woman.	*Snow White*
An animal that does something unusual	The hen Jack steals from the giant lays golden eggs.	*Jack and the Beanstalk*

board, and let the students identify the event correctly in order to roll the dice. Students also enjoy creating the themed gameboards themselves.

3. For older students: Discuss the symbolism represented in the story (e.g., the father's rage turns the brothers into ravens). Ask the students to research possible reasons why the brothers were turned into ravens instead of doves.

4. Toward the end of the story, the seventh raven appears with his left wing burned, his right wing broken and torn, and a small wound just under his heart. If it has not been done already during the class discussion, discuss with the students the association between the young girl's encounters with the sun (burned a hole in her eldest brother's shirt), the moon (tore a hole in his shirt), the stars (she stuck the glass bone into the shirt just under the spot near the heart), and the condition of the seventh raven.

Note: This activity is best as a short mini-lesson. The students can continue their discussion of fantasy and reality in their book discussion groups. A way to monitor their understanding of this concept is to ask them to write an example of fantasy and/or reality in their journals or reading logs. You can also ask them to share when they meet during the student/teacher conference. The overall tracking chart associated with different "magic" motifs can be added on to once or twice a week, or students may choose to write them on the chart as they find them.

Reproducible master 3.3 may be found at the end of this chapter.

CHARACTERISTIC: A CLEAR-CUT CHARACTERIZATION

The characters in the story are clearly good or evil, smart or stupid, or hard-working or lazy. By the end of the story, good has usually triumphed over evil, with the resulting happy ending for all the good characters.

Ed Young's beautifully illustrated *Yeh-Shen: A Cinderella Story from China* is retold by Ai-Ling Louie. It is the story of a young girl at the mercy of her stepmother and stepsister after the death of her father. The destruction of Yeh-Shen's beloved pet, a fish with golden eyes with which she shared her food, proves to be the downfall of the stepmother and stepsister. The bones of the fish provide Yeh-Shen with the golden slipper that ultimately unites her with the King of T'o Han. The king is so enamored of Yeh-Shen's beauty that he takes her as his wife. Because of their cruelty, the stepmother and stepsister are not allowed to join Yeh-Shen in the palace. Instead, they live the rest of their days in the cave home where they die in a shower of stones.

Summary: Yeh-Shen's kindness to her beloved pet is remembered and repaid. The stepmother's wicked acts to the young girl prevent her from living in the palace with Yeh-Shen and the king.

Lon Po Po: A Red-Riding Hood Story from China, retold by Ed Young, finds Shang, Tao, and Paotze living with their mother on the countryside of northern China. While the mother has gone to visit the Granny, the three children must outwit a wolf after he comes in acting as their Po Po (grandmother). The eldest daughter, Shang, convinces the wolf that he must pluck a ginkgo nut directly from the tree so that he can live forever. The wolf climbs into a basket to be pulled up into the tree with the girls. After two failed attempts to reach the ginkgo nuts find him falling to the ground, the wolf is coaxed into trying again. The wolf's hunger for the ginkgo nut, the girls, and immortality are to no avail as he plummets to the ground.

Summary: The mean, hungry wolf is outsmarted by good children.

Jan Brett's retelling and illustration of *Beauty and the Beast* is the classic love story. After Beauty's father plucks a rose from the Beast's garden, the father must either give up his life or have one of his daughters willingly live with the beast. It was Beauty's wish that he bring her the rose, so she insists on going to live with the Beast to save her father's life. The kindness and gentleness of the Beast soon helps Beauty to look past his ugliness. In the end, it is Beauty's love that breaks the spell of a meddlesome fairy. Beast, now a prince, takes Beauty as his bride.

> *Summary:* A young girl's love turns the Beast back into a handsome prince, thus breaking the spell of a meddlesome fairy.

FOCUS ACTIVITY: A CLEAR-CUT CHARACTERIZATION (GOOD OVER EVIL)

■ Characteristic: A clear-cut characterization
■ Activity: Character analysis
■ Summary: After completing a character trait analysis of a major character in the story, students will write a "Who am I?" riddle.
■ Materials: Folktales, Reproducible 3.4 (Character Trait Analysis Chart), construction paper

How Do You Do It?

Discuss with the class what is meant by a *trait* (e.g., a manner, custom, or feature that describes a character). Students must often be able to make inferences about characters in the story, therefore this is an important skill to aid in understanding the story. Questions that help students analyze the character's traits that sometimes must be inferred while reading the story are:

■ How does the character act in the story?
■ Are there any special features that set the character apart from the others?
■ What does the character say in the story?
■ What does the character think in the story?
■ What do these tell us about the character's personality?

Prepare a character trait analysis chart (see Figure 3.5 and Reproducible 3.4). Select a fairy tale to read together as a class, then analyze one of the major characters together as a class. List the traits that reflect the character (as shown in Figure 3.5). As students identify each trait, ask them also to state an example that supports the trait. A sample character trait analysis using *Rumpelstiltskin* by Paul O. Zelinsky is given in Figure 3.5.

It is important to discuss what the students heard in the story that supports each trait as being representative of the character. For example, if the students say Cinderella is kind, ask them what they heard, read, or saw (through illustrations) that told them so?

The next step is to let students select their own fairy tale to read. This works well in partners or individually. Students read the fairy tale, choose a character to analyze, and then record their responses. After students have completed this activity, bring them back to the large group to discuss the next step of writing riddles about the character. Refer to the character trait analysis done together as a class. The examples that illustrated the traits can be used to write a three- to four-line "Who am I?" riddle, such as the following:

Who Am I?

> *I spun three rooms full of straw into gold for the miller's daughter.*
> *I would only do it if she gave me her ring, necklace, and then promised me her baby when she became Queen.*
> *I rode around a fire in the woods on my wooden spoon crying out, "No one knows my name!"*
> *Can you guess who I am?*

FIGURE 3.5 Sample Character Trait Analysis Chart

TITLE OF STORY: *RUMPELSTILTSKIN* CHARACTER: RUMPELSTILTSKIN	
Trait	*Example*
1. Crafty	• The miller's daughter had to give him her necklace and ring, then promise him her baby so that he would spin each room full of straw into gold.
2. Hardworking	• He spun each of the three rooms full of straw into gold by the next morning.
3. Braggart	• He rode his cooking spoon around the fire in the woods as he cried out that no one knew his name.

The riddle works well using an 8½" × 11" piece of construction paper. The paper is folded in half to make the cover of a mini-book (see Figure 3.6). The student writes "Who am I?" on the front cover.

Inside the mini-book, the student writes the riddle on the left page of the book. He or she labels and draws a picture of the character on the right page of the book which is then covered with a flap of paper. On the outside of the paper flap, the student again writes, "Who am I?" (see Figure 3.7). The reader lifts the flap to reveal the character.

Students can share their riddles with the class. As students present their characters, write the names of the characters who are good on one side of the chalkboard, and the names of the characters who are evil or wicked on the other side of the board. After all have been presented, ask the students if they know how you have categorized the characters on the board. This leads into a discussion of the good versus evil characters and themes that are found in folktales—for example:

Snow White: beautiful, kind girl versus *wicked and jealous stepmother Queen*
Sleeping Beauty: beautiful princess versus *the wicked fairy*

Extensions
1. An interesting discussion that evolves from this analysis is the presentation of the characters regarding physical appearance. The good characters are shown as beautiful or handsome, whereas the evil characters often are not. Throughout the reading of the folktales, students may keep a list in

FIGURE 3.6 Folding Construction Paper in Half to Make a Mini-Book

WHO
AM
I?

Back Cover   Front Cover

**FIGURE 3.7   Inside of "Who Am I?"
Mini-Book**

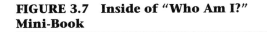

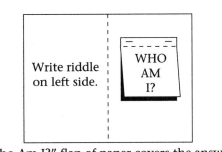

| Write riddle on left side. | WHO AM I? |

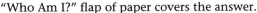

"Who Am I?" flap of paper covers the answer.

their journal of words that are used to describe or show how the good and evil characters in the story are depicted, as shown here:

	Good Characters	*Evil Characters*
Physical	Sweet	Mean
	Kind	Nasty
How they	Danced	Shrieked
talk/act	Sang	Furious

2. Students can keep a character journal by becoming one of the characters in the story they are reading. For instance, if a child "became" Jack from *Jack in the Beanstalk,* his or her journal entry might say:

Can you believe that guy? He must be nuts. I actually was able to trade him my cow for some magic beans. Wow, just think of all the possibilities. All of our problems will be solved. My mother and I won't have to go hungry again.

Note: The activity can be spread across three days:

Day One consists of the teacher reading the fairy tale aloud to the class. This is followed by a trait analysis of one to two characters in the story.

Day Two is when the students read their own fairy tale (in small groups, partners, or as individuals) and analyze the traits of a character in the story.

Day Three is when the teacher shows how to write the riddles using the character traits as an organizer for writing. Students create their own riddles to share with the class.

Reproducible master 3.4 may be found at the end of this chapter.

CHARACTERISTIC: THE USE OF REPETITION IN THE NARRATIVE

Repetition is a basic element in many folktale plots (Huck, Hepler, & Hickman, 1987). The numbers 3 and 7 are often repeated in folktales. For example, there are three little pigs in *The Three Little Pigs* and three wishes in *The Fisherman and His Wife,* and seven dwarves in *Snow White and the Seven Dwarves.* In addition, the repetition of patterns is often present—for example, "Fee fi fo fum" in *Jack and the Beanstalk* and "Mirror, mirror, on the wall" in *Snow White.* This repetition of phrases may take the form of responses, chants, or poems.

Jan Brett's version of *Goldilocks and the Three Bears* follows Goldilocks through the home of the three bears as she samples their three bowls of steaming porridge that are too hot, too cold, and then just right; their three chairs that are too hard, too soft, and then just right; and their three beds that are too high at the head, too high at the foot, and then just right. Throughout the story, the phrases the "great, huge bear" and "his rough, great voice," the "middle-sized bear" and "her middle voice," and "small, wee bear" and "little, small, wee voice" are repeated. When the bears return home, they are bewildered to find things in their home not quite the way they left them. As they notice their bowls of porridge, the repetition of "Somebody has been at my porridge" is repeated by each bear. The small, wee bear follows suit adding on, " . . . and has eaten it all up." This repetitive sequence is maintained as the bears move through their house noticing their chairs, their beds, and finally Goldilocks.

Summary: A family of three bears goes for a walk in the woods. Goldilocks enters their house and samples their three bowls of porridge, three chairs, and three beds.

Jon Scieszka and Lane Smith tell the story of the three little pigs from the wolf's perspective in their book, *The True Story of the 3 Little Pigs*. In this version, the wolf visits the houses of the three little pigs in order to borrow a cup of sugar for his "dear old granny's birthday cake." At the first pig's house, he calls out with, "Little pig, little pig, are you in?" and changes to "Mr. Pig, Mr. Pig, are you in?" when he visits the second and third pigs. "I huffed, and I puffed, and sneezed a great sneeze" is also followed loosely, since the format changes slightly as the wolf visits each pig.

Summary: The "true" story involves a cup of sugar, a head cold, and a bad reputation for which the wolf is known. The wolf goes to visit his three pig neighbors as he looks to borrow a cup of sugar. Each visit, the wolf is overcome with a sneezing fit where he huffs and puffs with great vigor. Accompanied by a reporter, three police pigs arrive to take the wolf into custody.

FOCUS ACTIVITY: THE USE OF REPETITION IN THE NARRATIVE

◼ Characteristic: The use of repetition in the narrative
◼ Activity: Writing song lyrics
◼ Summary: Students analyze a fairy tale to determine elements that are repeated throughout the story.
◼ Materials: Fairy tales, paper, pencil, Reproducible 3.5 (Repetitive Patterns)

How Do You Do It?

Before reading, discuss with the class what is meant by *repetition* (e.g., to do again). Point out how there is often repetition of the numbers or phrases within the folktales. Using *Goldilocks and the Three Bears* by Jan Brett, ask the students to listen for repetitive patterns in the story. After reading, determine if there are any repetitive numbers or phrases that are maintained throughout the story. Here are two examples:

◼ In *Goldilocks and the Three Bears*, there are three bears, three bowls, three chairs, and three beds.
◼ The phrases "great, huge bear," "middle-sized bear," and "small, wee bear" are heard throughout the story.

Once these elements have been identified (see Figure 3.8), the students can work in groups, select a folktale to read, analyze for patterns, and then share with the rest of the class. The information can be recorded using a chart format that can be a later reference if students decide to transform a folktale or write their own. Use Reproducible 3.5 as a record sheet for the students. As the students continue reading folktales throughout this study, they can record patterns of numbers and phrases that are found.

FIGURE 3.8   Identifying Repetitive Patterns Found in the Story

REPETITIVE PATTERNS		
Story	*Numbers*	*Phrases*
Goldilocks and the Three Bears by Jan Brett	Three bears Three bowls Three chairs Three beds	great, huge bear middle-sized bear small, wee bear
The True Story of the 3 Little Pigs by Jon Scieszka and Lane Smith	Three pigs Three houses Three cops	huffed and puffed sneezed a great sneeze

Extension

The students can write songs using the repetitive patterns found in their folktale. The following song, for instance, can be sung to the tune of "My Bonnie Lies over the Ocean." It highlights the repetition of the number 3 heard throughout the story of *Goldilocks and the Three Bears*. This particular song is sung without the chorus:

> *The bears went into the woods,*
> *They went together, all three.*
> *They were waiting for their porridge to cool,*
> *They were to return very soon.*

The children might decide to focus on one area (e.g., the repetition of the number 3) or use all of the elements together. In the following example, the fairy tale is sung to the tune of "Three Blind Mice." Again, the use of the number 3 is emphasized:

> *Three brown bears.*
> *Three brown bears.*
> *Went off into the woods.*
> *Went off into the woods.*
> *They returned to their house and found it not right,*
> *Three bowls, three chairs, three beds were a sight.*
> *And who do you think was out like a light?*
> *Gol-di-locks,*
> *Gol-di-locks.*

When doing this activity for the first time, it is best to write several of the stanzas together as a group. Once the students have the general idea, then additional stanzas can be created by asking different groups to work on particular episodes from the story. Have them write their stanzas on a transparency, then the whole class will be able to sing it together when they meet back together and share as a whole class.

After doing it together as a class, the students may choose to do their own fairy tale analysis. Remind them to look for instances of repetition involving phrases and the numbers 3 or 7. If you keep a file of familiar songs and tunes for the students to access, they can use these as a resource when creating their own tunes. For some students, doing multiple stanzas will be a breeze, but others will perhaps feel more comfortable working with group or partner support. Older students may want to write their verses using more popular music. Students can illustrate their verses for a big book.

Note: This activity can be broken into a three-day lesson:

Day One would consist of the class working together in a large group and/or small groups to create stanzas for a common folktale.

Day Two follows with the students selecting a folktale, then working in small groups or partners to write their own song. Depending on the age level and ability level of the students, it may be necessary to extend this portion of the activity over several days. Students who finish early could write and illustrate their folktales.

Day Three involves the groups sharing their songs.

Reproducible master 3.5 may be found at the end of this chapter.

Writing Your Own Folktales

Connecting the reading of folktales with the writing of folktales is discussed through two different activities. Writing transformations of favorite folktales is a fun way for students to play with changing aspects of story elements related to the characteristics and motifs of folktales.

Calmenson's book, *The Principal's New Clothes*, changes the classic story of *The Emperor's New Clothes* to a modern-day character and setting where the emperor is now Mr. Bundy, the principal at P.S. 88. The basic storyline remains the same as the vanity of the principal, like the emperor, almost becomes his undoing. The students utilize their knowledge of characteristics and motifs to aid them as they make decisions about story transformations.

The second activity is an opportunity for the students to assume the role of a character from one of their stories by corresponding in a letter format. Their knowledge of a particular story's elements (e.g., character, setting, problem, events, and solution) will serve as background information when corresponding with each other. Two stages of the writing process that are the central focus in these two activities are prewriting and drafting (see Figure 3.9).

FOCUS ACTIVITY: TRANSFORMING FOLKTALES
▨ Activity: Writing transformation stories
▨ Summary: The students will take a folktale they have read in class, and write a new story that parallels an old story.
▨ Materials: Hans Christian Andersen's *The Emperor's New Clothes*, Stephanie Calmenson's *The Principal's New Clothes*, Reproducible 3.6 (Story Map), Reproducible 3.7 (Venn Diagram), Reproducible 3.8 (Transformations), Reproducible 3.9 (Story Checklist)

The section that follows discusses the use of collaborative group writing as a way of modeling the writing process (revisit Chapter 2). Tompkins (1998) discusses the use of class collaboration as a way of introducing the writing process. The teacher acts as a guide, modeling the process the students will move through, just like published authors do. The benefit of this technique is that students are able to practice the process approach to writing in a supportive environment.

How Do You Do It?

The focus of this part of the activity is on prewriting:

FIGURE 3.9   Writing Stage with Corresponding Activities Related to Folktales

WRITING STAGE	ACTIVITY	
	Transformations	*Letter Writing*
Prewriting	(1) ■ Analyzing a folktale —Story map —Venn diagram ■ Deciding what elements will be transformed	(1) ■ Choosing a partner ■ Becoming a character
Drafting	(2) ■ Using the transformation map as a guide while writing	(2) ■ Writing letters with a partner by becoming a character
Conferencing for Content	(3) ■ Using a checklist	
→Revising	→Making changes	
Conferencing for Conventions	(4) ■ Checking for capitalization, usage, punctuation, and spelling	
→Revising	→Making changes	
Publishing	(5) ■ Making a class big book	

STAGE OF THE WRITING PROCESS

Prewriting   ■ Analyzing a folktale

—Story map

—Venn diagram

■ Deciding what elements will be transformed

Introduce students to the following two books by reading them aloud together and discussing basic elements of each story:

Hans Christian Andersen's *The Emperor's New Clothes*

Stephanie Calmenson's *The Principal's New Clothes*

Ask students to listen for the following elements:

- ■ *Characters:*   Who are the most important people in the story?
- ■ *Setting:*   Where does the story take place?
- ■ *Problem:*   What stands in the way of the character—possibly an obstacle, dilemma, or challenge?
- ■ *Events:*   What are the most important happenings in the story?
- ■ *Solution:*   How is the obstacle, dilemma, or challenge settled by the end of the story?

After reading the first book, map the story on a story map. Repeat the process with the second book. An example of a story map of Calmenson's book is shown in Figure 3.10 (see also Reproducible 3.6).

Next, students can work in small groups, partners, or individually to create a Venn diagram that compares and contrasts the two stories. Allow time for sharing of each Venn diagram in order to create a class diagram that incorpo-

FIGURE 3.10 Story Map of Calmenson's Book, *The Principal's New Clothes*

THE PRINCIPAL'S NEW CLOTHES	
Characters	■ Mr. Bundy, the principal ■ Moe and Ivy, suit makers
Setting	■ P.S. (Public School) 88
Problem	■ Moe and Ivy try to pull a con job on the principal. They tell him the special suit cannot be seen by anyone who is not good at his or her job or who is just plain stupid.
Events	■ Mr. Bundy has so many suits that sometimes he changes at lunchtime to show off. ■ Moe and Ivy want to make Mr. Bundy a suit with special powers. ■ Mr. Bundy sent his vice principal and the smartest student to see the suit, but they didn't want to tell him they didn't see anything at all. ■ Mr. Bundy went to look and didn't see anything. ■ Moe and Ivy deliver the suit for Mr. Bundy to wear to the morning assembly. ■ Mr. Bundy paid Moe and Ivy. ■ Everyone raved about the clothes, and Mr. Bundy thought he was the only person who was stupid.
Solution	■ A kindergartner yells out, "The principal's in his underwear." ■ Everyone passed clothes to Mr. Bundy for him to wear.

rates all of the students' suggestions. This leads into a discussion of how Calmenson's story parallels Andersen's story (see Figure 3.11 and Reproducible 3.7). Students then choose a folktale they would like to transform. Suggestions for ways to transform a story include:

- ■ Make the language more modern.
- ■ Change the characters.
- ■ Change the setting.
- ■ Change some of the events.
- ■ Tell the story from a different point of view.
- ■ Reverse the roles of the characters.
- ■ Continue where the story left off.

Students choose one to two elements to transform using the following format (see Figure 3.12 and Reproducible 3.8):

FIGURE 3.11 Partial Venn Diagram Comparing/Contrasting Two Stories

THE PRINCIPAL'S NEW CLOTHES & THE EMPEROR'S NEW CLOTHES	
Different	*Different*
Takes place in a school	Takes place in a castle
A principal is the main character	An emperor is the main character
Alike	
Both the principal and the emperor get conned into thinking they will have clothes with special powers	

FIGURE 3.12 Identifying Story Elements That Will Be Transformed

---

Story to be Transformed: *The Emperor's New Clothes*

1. I will transform the story by changing...

   _____the emperor (major character)_____

   to the President of the United States of _____

   America. _____

2. I will transform the story by changing...

   _____the castle (setting)_____

   to the White House in Washington, D.C. _____

3. I will transform the story by changing...

   _____the two tailors (villains)_____

   to the Speaker of the House and the Senate Majority _____

   Leader. _____

▪ Write the two to three elements that you will transform onto the story map, then complete the other elements of the story map (characters, setting, problem, events, and solution).

▪ Use the story map as your plan for writing, and let it guide in the drafting of your story.

Mini-Lesson

Read a folktale to the class. Work with the students to select three aspects of the story that could be changed. Groups of students could be responsible for thinking of one aspect each. Ask the groups to share the different transformations they chose.

The next stage of the writing process is drafting:

STAGE OF THE WRITING PROCESS

Drafting   ▪ Using the transformation map as a guide while writing

Using the transformation map as a guide, the students can now write their own transformation story. Some students may feel more comfortable sketching out a story map to use in conjunction with their transformation map. When they are done drafting, they can use these maps to examine their papers to be sure the critical elements of the stories are included.

Mini-Lesson

Using the folktale for which the class brainstormed three transformations, discuss how the story could be extended to write a class folktale. Model writing a rough draft on the overhead by asking questions and soliciting advice from the students. Show how the use of editing marks (see Figure 3.13) is helpful when adding or deleting information to a draft (e.g., the use of a caret to show an insert).

FIGURE 3.13 Editing Marks

Mark	Symbol	Example
Delete	ℐ	~~She~~ Carla screamed hysterically.
Insert	⅄	Carla screamed hysterically ^at him.
Indent paragraph	¶ or →	→When a Killer Whale is born, it is about seven feet long. Males grow to about thirty feet long but females grow to only half that size.
Capitalize	☰	She shouted at ḵaren.
Change to lower case	/	Why did I Ȧsk Bobby to dance?
Add period	⊙	My notebook is missing⊙
Add comma	⊙	The dog⸲ cat⸲ and rabbit slept together.
Add apostrophe	⊙	He couldn't wait for the movie to start.

FIGURE 3.14 Checklist for Reviewing the Story

CHECKLIST FOR REVIEWING THE STORY	
Do I have the kind of lead that grabs the reader's attention?	Comments:
Does my story have a beginning, middle, and end?	Comments:
What kinds of words did I use to make the story more interesting?	Comments:
Does the story that I have written make sense?	Comments:
What transformations were used to change the story?	Comments:
Are there any details that could be added that would enhance the story?	Comments:
Is there a good closing at the end of the story, or is the reader left thinking, "What?"	Comments:

Next is conferencing for content:

STAGE OF THE WRITING PROCESS

Conferencing for content   ■ Using a checklist

Work with the students to review the group story using the checklist shown in Figure 3.14 (see also Reproducible 3.9).

After the group has talked about the story via the checklist, ask the students to work in small groups to talk about one way they could make each of the elements that needed improvement better. For example, if they found the lead needs some work, then each group could brainstorm ways to improve the lead. A great way to look at leads is to use the work of other authors to show how it was done effectively. In some cases, the students may find they do not like the lead that was used by the author. Either way, it encourages them to think critically about what they consider to be "good" writing.

Once the groups have finished brainstorming (5 to 10 minutes), then bring the groups back together to share possible improvements that could be made to the story. This also provides another opportunity for the teacher and students to utilize the editing marks to add in information to the story. Once the class has agreed that the story is completed, then it could be made into a big book. Groups of students could take portions of the text and rewrite it on regular paper first. This allows them the opportunity to check for the correct use of conventions of language:

STAGE OF THE WRITING PROCESS

Conferencing for conventions   ■ Checking for capitalization, usage, punctuation, and spelling

The students can swap pages to check for use of mechanics. General guidelines that could be listed on chart paper or overhead could include the following:

- ■ Are capitals used correctly?
- ■ Are punctuation marks used correctly?
- ■ Is each word spelled correctly?
- ■ Are the words in the story used correctly?
- ■ Do the sentences sound correct?
- ■ Is the handwriting neat and legible?

Once the groups are satisfied that all of the conventions of language are present, they can then proceed to write the final copy:

STAGE OF THE WRITING PROCESS

Publishing   ■ Making a class big book

Groups finishing first could be responsible for creating the cover of the book. The final pages with illustrations could be organized into the big book format. *Reminder:* Be sure to share the big book with another class or display it in the library.

Note: Here is a brief summary on children writing their own folktales:

Days One and Two consist of the class analyzing the two folktales for story elements and comparing/contrasting the two stories.

Days Three and Four involve the students selecting a folktale they would like to transform, identifying the elements to be changed, and writing a draft of their story. This portion of the activity may need to be extended longer to allow enough time for the students to draft.

Days Five through Seven consist of modeling how to conference for content followed by adding or deleting information to help improve the story. Follow the same process with conferencing for conventions.

Days Eight and Nine are necessary so that students have the opportunity to fine-tune their draft and illustrate it.

Reminder: This section discusses how the students move through the stages of the writing process. Other stages of this process will be discussed in more depth in Chapters 4 and 5. However, once the draft is completed, students should have the option of moving ahead without waiting for the others. It is not uncommon for writers to return to a previous stage to rethink what has been done so far. (See Chapter 2 concerning the recursivity of the writing process.) For example, a student in the editing for conventions conference may get some additional ideas for developing content of the draft, even though the focus was not on content but on grammar. The student would then take another look at the draft to make the content revisions as well as convention revisions also noted during the conference.

Reproducible masters 3.6–3.9 may be found at the end of this chapter.

FOCUS ACTIVITY: LETTER WRITING

- ▨ Activity: Character writing
- ▨ Summary: Students first choose a partner with whom to work, then decide what two major characters from a folktale each will become. The students use the characters' roles to correspond in a letter format back and forth with each other.
- ▨ Materials: Friendly letter forms, posterboard, construction paper, tagboard, three-ring binder, folktales to use as reference, Reproducible 3.10 (Letter Writing)

How Do You Do It?

The focus is on the prewriting stage of writing where students choose a partner to correspond in a letter format:

STAGE OF THE WRITING PROCESS

Prewriting   ▨ Choosing a partner

                    ▨ Becoming a character

Introduce the "friendly letter" format to the students who will be working on this project. Elements of a friendly letter are shown in Figure 3.15 (see also Reproducible 3.10). Explain the format, then model for the students how to become a character by using what they know about the book and adding other information to make the letter more interesting. Students can refer to previous story maps or Venn diagrams they used when analyzing the folktales they read. Using *Jack and the Beanstalk*, the major characters are Jack and the Ogre:

April 1

369 Beanstalk Drive
Green Bean, USA 12345

Dear Ogre,

    I couldn't believe my eyes! I woke up, and outside my window was a huge beanstalk reaching up into the sky. As soon as I dressed, I ran outside and began to climb the beanstalk. Finally, I climbed through the clouds and saw your castle. I think I'll come for a visit.

Just thought I'd warn you,

Jack

FIGURE 3.15 Letter Format

April 16
(DATE)

1234 Road
Enchanted Forest, USA 09876
(HEADING)

Dear Rapunzel, (GREETING)

    When I was riding through the forest, I heard your voice carried by the wind. I kept looking for you everywhere, but I couldn't seem to find you. Please give me a clue that will aid in my search. (BODY)

Faithfully yours,
(CLOSING)

The Prince
(SIGNATURE)

April 7

158 Skyhigh Ave.
Cloud City, USA 54321

Dear Jack,

    I don't think that would be a wise move. Why, just last night I ate a tasty little boy…JUST LIKE YOU! In fact, that is my favorite meal of all. Heh, heh, heh. Just kidding! Come on over. I'd love to have you for a visit. Heh, heh, heh.

Love to have you over,

Ogre

Mini-Lesson

Select two other characters from a familiar folktale, and ask students to take turns adding in lines to the letter as their responses are written for everyone to see (e.g., use large chart paper or overhead).

    After students are familiar with the format of the letter, ask them to choose a partner with whom they will correspond by writing letters. The two partners each select two different characters from the same folktale and exchange names and addresses. Once this has been done, all oral communication between the two partners are completed. From that point on, their interactions are to take place through the letters they write to each other:

STAGE OF THE WRITING PROCESS

Drafting   ■ Writing letters with a partner by becoming a character

Rules to follow for this assignment are:

■ Do not speak to each other.
■ All contact takes place through writing only.
■ The writing must be in letter format.

- Letters must be mailed through the classroom post office.
- Response letters must be mailed within two days of having received letter from partner.
- Partners are to exchange at least five letters apiece.

Once all of the letters have been mailed, and the students have corresponded together, then the two partners can polish their "drafts" to make them into a big book or regular-sized book. Walk the students through conferencing for content and then conferencing for conventions, using the same process that was followed in writing the transformation story.

The two facing pages inside the book could consist of the letter on the left page and an illustration of the letter on the right page. Posterboard cut in half works well as the front and back cover, with tagboard or 8½" × 14" construction paper as the inside pages. Books can be bound easily with a three-ring binder on the left side at the top, middle, and bottom of the book.

Students can examine other books to look at how they are put together. Items to consider when making the big book include:

- Front cover
- Title page
- Copyright
- Dedication page
- Table of contents
- Page numbers
- Author's page

The completed book can be shared with the rest of the class before being added to the classroom library. If students elect to send their writing off for other publication, then they can make a smaller version of the big book to do so.

Extension

Students can use what they learned when they transformed folktales to write their letters. Students choose two to three elements to transform, then map out the rest of the plan they will follow. This would be a collaborative effort up until this point. After the transformations have been agreed upon, the oral communication stops and written communication through letters begins.

Note: Set aside two weeks for this activity:

Day One introduces the letter format to the students, students selecting letter writing partners, and determining which folktale character each student will be.

Days Two through Seven give the students enough time to exchange several entries. The number of days can easily be lengthened to extend over several weeks to allow the students ample time to write and respond as that character.

Days Eight through Ten involve the students taking the drafts of their correspondence and coordinating it into a big book.

Reproducible 3.10 may be found at the end of this chapter.

Tieing in to Technology

INTERNET CONNECTIONS

The Internet offers a wealth of resources about folk literature that is readily available to the teacher and students. Students can visit the web site of the de Grummond Collection at the University of Southern Mississippi:

■ http://www.lib.usm.edu.~degrum/tales.htm
This site contains information pertaining to *The Cinderella Project* and *The Little Red Riding Hood Project.* The two projects are image and text archives containing various versions of the fairy tales. There are 12 Cinderella stories and 16 Little Red Riding Hood stories in English language versions published during the eighteenth, nineteenth, and twentieth centuries. *Jack and the Beanstalk* and *Jack the Giant Killer, Sleeping Beauty,* and *Snow White* are also available in numerous translations and adaptations. The students can easily print out different versions to compare the similarities and differences across various cultures.

Other interesting sites where the students can access folktales include:

■ http://www.pacificnet.net/~johnr/aesop/aesophca.html
This contains links to the work of Hans Christian Andersen: *The Little Match Girl, The Emperor's New Suit, Little Tiny* or *Thumbelina,* and *The Tinder-box.*
■ http://www.scils.rutgers.edu/special/kay/snowwhite.html
Kay Vandergrift's web page, which includes various information about Snow White, is a useful teacher resource. Read about films, videos, and recordings of Snow White, or read a hypertext version that provides links to 36 alternative editions of the tale. Vandergrift also provides a link to other resources in folklore, mythology, and fairy tales.

PUBLISHING

There are many different publishing programs available that enable students to create using a variety of formats. The process of creating and publishing such texts puts children in situations where they are engaged in public writing with a strong sense of their aims and audiences (Downes & Fatouros, 1995). Some possibilities include:

■ After reading *The Principal's New Clothes* by Stephanie Calmenson, create an invitation that asks guests to attend a gathering where the principal will unveil his new suit.
■ Design a "Most Wanted" flier that offers a reward for the capture of the Snow Queen in the story by P. J. Lynch.
■ Students can also publish stories they write on the World Wide Web: http://www.kidpub.org/kidpub/ This site offers a detailed description of how to send stories to KidPub as well as a form that can be used to submit the story. Another link is the Kidpub Publisher's top picks of their favorite stories and poems that have been submitted.

VIDEOTAPING

Students can write a script based on one of the stories they have read, transform a story, or create an original script using the elements of the genre to guide them. The script can be videotaped to make a film version of their screenplay. *Camcorder in the Classroom: Using the Videocamera to Enliven Curriculum* by Adrienne L. Herrell and Joel P. Fowler, Jr., is one resource to help guide this process. Possibilities for writing screenplays (scripts) directly from the folktale could include:

- *Jack and the Beanstalk* has three basic settings that include Jack's house, the beanstalk, and the giant's castle. Using these backdrops as a base, the students can write the screenplay to move back and forth between the three settings. Major scenes can then be written around these settings.
- A script for *Little Red Riding Hood* could revolve around Little Red on her way through the forest to visit her grandmother. Her initial meeting with the wolf would take place there in the forest, and then it could jump forward to Grandmother's house for the rest of the story.

CONCEPT OVERLAYS

A concept keyboard is an alternative input device that may be used instead of, or as well as, the standard computer keyboard. It is an A3-size touch-sensitive board divided into 128 cells, each of which sends a signal to the computer when pressed (Downes & Fatouros, 1995). Cells can be linked to adjacent cells or programmed separately. This allows the size and shape of response areas to vary. The overlays can be used to show what letter, word, or phrase each response represents. When a word or phrase is selected, the response will appear on the computer screen. *Intellikeys* (Macintosh, Windows, DOS) is one publisher of concept keyboard software. Consider this possibility:

- Groups of students can design a concept overlay that would enable others to create a summary of the story. Major words on the concept overlay for *Goldilocks and the Three Bears* could include *Goldilocks, Papa Bear, Mama Bear, Baby Bear, hot, cold, just right, hard, soft,* and so forth. With the inclusion of each letter of the alphabet, words such as *a, and, was,* and *the* can be easily added into the story shown on the computer monitor. A graphic representation of the character can also be shown on the same key as the word (i.e., Goldilocks).

DATABASE CONSTRUCTION

Students can construct a database of information to help keep track of various aspects of the folktales they have read. Major categories could be as follows:

- Use various motifs, such as a long sleep or enchantment, the use of magical powers, magical transformations, the presence of magical objects, the granting of wishes, and the use of trickery.
- Review suggestions in Huck, Hepler, and Hickman (1987). Each folktale could have information pertaining to opening and ending conversations, origin of the tale, clues to the country of origin, talents of the characters, tasks to be done, verses, refrains, chants, illustrations, and special or unique categories.

Annotated Bibliography: Folktales

Brett, Jan. (1987). *Goldilocks and the Three Bears*. New York: G. P. Putnam's Sons.
Goldilocks makes herself at home in the house of the three bears by sampling their bowls of porridge, sitting in their chairs, and testing the comfort of their beds. When the bears return home from a walk in the woods, they find Goldilocks asleep in the small, wee bear's bed.

Calmenson, Stephanie. (1989). *The Principal's New Clothes*. New York: Scholastic.
This story is the modern version of *The Emperor's New Clothes*. The joke is on Mr. Bundy when he falls victim to Moe and Ivy after deciding to get a new suit and finds out how capable his teachers and students really are.

Carle, Eric. (1988). *Eric Carle's Treasury of Classic Stories for Children by Aesop, Hans Christian Andersen and the Brothers Grimm*. New York: Orchard Books.
Some of the folktales included in Carle's collection are "Tom Thumb," "The Fishermen and His Wife," and "The Seven Swabians."

Climo, Shirley. (1989). *The Egyptian Cinderella*. New York: HarperCollins.
Climo bases this story from one first recorded by the Roman historian Strabo in the first century B.C. Rhodopis, a slave from Greece, is destined to become the wife of the Pharaoh after a falcon drops one of her rose-red slippers into his lap. Illustrations are by Ruth Heller.

Climo, S. (1993). *The Korean Cinderella*. New York: HarperCollins.
Climo combines three versions of a Korean tale to tell of a heroine who is a dutiful daughter, who prevails over an unkind stepmother and stepsister, and who is rescued from her life by an honorable official. Heller's illustrations are based on information gathered at museums and palaces, at festivals and concerts, and at a village set up to replicate the way Korean people lived 300 years ago.

Geringer, Laura. (1994). *The Seven Ravens*. New York: HarperCollins.
A young girl searches for her seven brothers who were turned into ravens after a curse is cast on them by their father.

Hague, Michael. (1989). *Cinderella and Other Tales from Perrault*. New York: Henry Holt.
Seven of Charles Perrault's folktales. Stories include "The Sleeping Beauty," "Little Red Riding Hood," "Blue Beard," "Master Cat" or "Puss 'n' Boots," "The Fairies," "Cinderella," "Riquet with the Tuft," and "Tom Thumb."

Howe, John. (1998). *Jack and the Beanstalk*. Boston: Little, Brown.
Jack sells the family cow for a handful of magic beans that grow into a beanstalk reaching high into the sky. Jack climbs the beanstalk three times to the giant's world, taking the hen that lays golden eggs, a bag of gold, and a magical harp. The giant pursues Jack on the third trip, and Jack must cut down the beanstalk with an ax to save his own life and kill the giant.

Jeffers, Susan. (1980). *Hansel and Gretel*. New York: Dial Books.
This is a classic Brothers Grimm tale of the brother and sister's triumph over the evils they encounter after their mother convinces their father to desert them.

Lynch, P. J. (1994). *The Snow Queen*. New York: Harcourt Brace.
Retold from the original English version by Caroline Peachey, this is Hans Christian Andersen's story of a young girl's attempts to save her friend from the Snow Queen. Journeying to the garden of the enchantress, Gerda determines to save her beloved friend, Kay, after he vanishes one winter day. Gerda battles the magic of the Snow Queen to free Kay, alone and blue with cold on a frozen lake bed, and win back his heart.

Marks, Alan. (1989). *The Fisherman and His Wife*. Saxonville, MA: Picture Book Studio.
This is a tale from the Brothers Grimm of a humble fisherman, his greedy wife, and a magical fish. After the fisherman throws the fish back into the sea, his wife sends him back repeatedly to ask the fish to make her grander and more powerful. After asking the fish to make her king, emperor, Pope, and "to be like God," the fish rewards the wife's greediness by restoring her back to her original shack by the sea.

Marshall, James. (1987). *Red Riding Hood*. New York: Dial Books,
The "charming and urbane" wolf Red Riding Hood meets on her way to Grandma's turns out to have more than friendship on his mind. When Red Riding Hood and Grandma wind up as dinner and dessert, their only hope is rescue by a passing hunter.

Mayer, Marianna. (1994). *Baba Yaga and Vasilisa the Brave.* New York: Morrow Books.
This classic Russian folktale features the beautiful orphan Vasilisa, her jealous step-mother and stepsisters, and the witch Baba Yaga. With the help of her doll made from her true mother's love, Vasilisa manages to outwit Baba Yaga and her step-mother and stepsisters. She is taken in by an elderly woman who shows Vasilisa's beautiful fabrics to the Tsar who, in turn, falls in love with Vasilisa.

Pearson, Susan. (1989). *Jack and the Beanstalk.* New York: Simon and Schuster.
In this version, Jack climbs the beanstalk to the giant's world, taking a bag of gold, a singing harp, and a hen that lays golden eggs. With the giant fast on his heels, Jack narrowly escapes down the beanstalk.

Rogasky, Barbara. (1982). *Rapunzel.* New York: Holiday House.
A husband and wife must promise their first-born child to the witch after he is caught stealing rampion from her garden. The witch locks the child, Rapunzel, in a tall tower where she is found and rescued by a handsome prince. Illustrations are done by Tricia Schart Hyman.

Sage, Alison. (1990). *Rumpelstiltskin.* New York: Dial Books.
Rose, a poor miller's daughter, must spin straw into gold for the king. A mysterious little man offers to do the task in exchange for her first-born child. When he returns to collect his due, Rose is offered a second chance, so she must guess the little man's name in order to save her baby.

Schroeder, Alan. (1994). *Lily and the Wooden Bowl.* New York: Doubleday Books.
This story tells of how Lily kept her promise to her grandmother to never remove a lacquered bowl from her head, which was placed there to hide Lily's beauty from the world.

Scieszka, Jon. (1989). *The True Story of the 3 Little Pigs.* New York: Penguin Books.
This is a retelling of "The Three Little Pigs" from the wolf's perspective. A Wolf shares the real story that started with a birthday cake for his dear old granny and ended with the wolf being thrown in jail. He earnestly states his conviction that he was framed.

Vuong, Lynette Dyer. (1982). *The Brocaded Slipper and Other Vietnamese Tales.* New York: HarperCollins.
Five stories from Vietnam include explanatory notes from the author and a guide to pronouncing Vietnamese names included in the stories. Included are "The Brocaded Slipper," "Little Finger of the Watermelon Patch," "The Fairy Grotto," "Master Frog," and "The Lampstand Princess."

3.1 Story Events for Plot Graph

Title of Story:
1.
2.
3.
4.
5.
6.
7.
8.
9.
10.

3.2 Plot Graph with Key

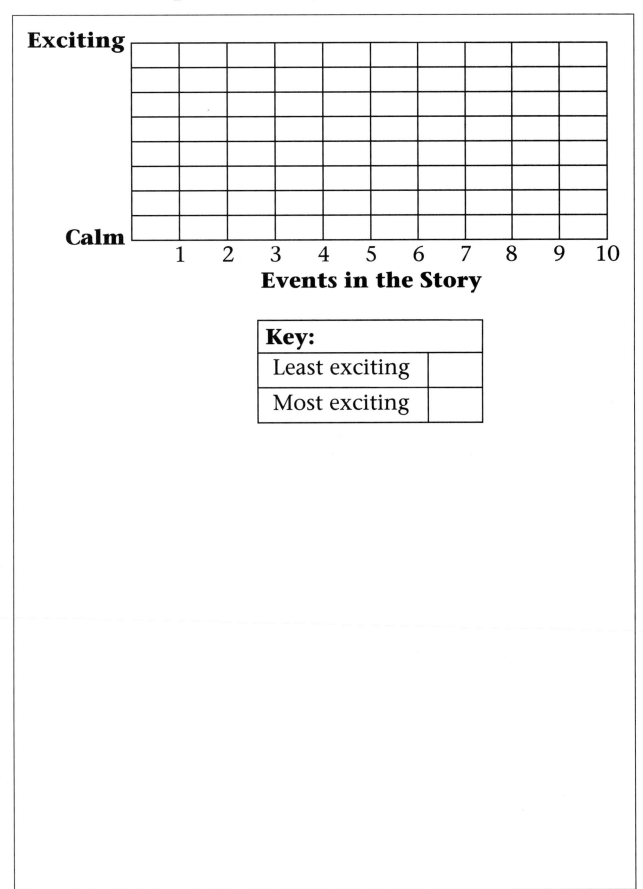

3.3 Magic Scavenger Hunt

Find an example of each category, and list the story from which it was found.

What Did You Find?	Example	Where Did You Find It?
An object used to protect the character		
A "good" character who changes form		
An animal that tricks a character		
A character who grants wishes		
An "evil" character who changes form		
A character who must make a journey of some kind		
A character who has magical powers		
An animal that does something unusual		

3.4 Character Trait Analysis Chart

Title of Story:	
Character:	
Trait	Example
1.	▪ ▪
2.	▪ ▪
3.	▪ ▪

3.5 Repetitive Patterns Record Sheet

Read the story. Look for numbers or phrases that repeat. Write the numbers or phrases on this record sheet.

Repetitive Patterns		
Title of Story	Numbers	Phrases

3.6 Story Map
After reading the folktale, identify the story elements.

Title of Story:	
Characters	
Setting	
Problem	
Events	
Solution	

3.7   Venn Diagram

Directions: Compare and contrast the two different versions of the folktale you read.

Title of Story #1:	Title of Story #2:
Different	Different
Alike	

3.8 Transformations

Check (✓) two to three items to be changed in the story:

□ Make the language more modern.
□ Change the characters.
□ Change the setting.
□ Change some of the events.
□ Tell the story from a different point of view.
□ Reverse the roles of the characters.
□ Continue where the story left off.

1. I will transform the story by changing...

   _____

   to _____

   _____

   _____

   _____

2. I will transform the story by changing...

   _____

   to _____

   _____

   _____

   _____

3. I will transform the story by changing...

   _____

   to _____

   _____

   _____

   _____

3.9 Story Checklist

Checklist for Reviewing the Story	
Do I have the kind of lead that grabs the reader's attention?	Comments:
Does my story have a beginning, middle, and end?	Comments:
What kinds of words did I use to make the story more interesting?	Comments:
Does the story that I have written make sense?	Comments:
What transformations were used to change the story?	Comments:
Are there any details that could be added that would enhance the story?	Comments:
Is there a good closing at the end of the story, or is the reader left thinking, "What?"	Comments:

3.10 Letter Writing

_____

_____
_____
_____
_____

_____
_____
_____
_____
_____
_____
_____
_____
_____
_____
_____

_____

_____

chapter 4

All about Fables

What Is a Fable?

A fable is a brief didactic tale, in which animals, or occasionally the elements, speak as human beings (Huck, Hepler, & Hickman, 1987; Abrahamson, 1995). It is a brief narrative that takes abstract ideas of behavior—good or bad, wise or foolish—and attempts to make them concrete and striking enough to be understood and remembered (Sutherland, 1997). The characters' actions in fables revolve on a single event that teaches a moral. The contribution of fables to our literary heritage is in how they have affected our attitudes toward moral and ethical problems (Sutherland, 1997).

Fabulists

People who write fables are known as *fabulists*. If you say *fables* to English-speaking children, they think at once of Aesop; to French children, La Fontaine and *fables* are inseparably associated; and in Asia, it is *The Panchatantra, The Fables of Bidpai,* or the *Jatakas* (Sutherland, 1997). Of these, only the fables of Aesop and La Fontaine are considered to be appropriate for children, and, in most cases, best if used with older children due to the didactic wisdom and complexity represented within the fable.

Aesop

Though it is doubted by some whether Aesop did, in fact, exist, he is said to have been a Greek slave who lived between 620 and 560 B.C. (Bosma, 1987;

Huck, Hepler, & Hickman, 1987; Sutherland, 1997). The fables of Aesop are written in narrative form consisting of a character, a single action, and a moral. His lessons are directed toward manipulating external forces and controlling or overcoming enemies (Bosma, 1987).

La Fontaine

La Fontaine, *le fablier* (the fable-teller), wrote his fables in verse (Sutherland, 1997). His fables are similar to the tales of Aesop, since they maintain the shortness of length, animal characters, and single event pointing to a specific moral. Due to the similarity between the two, it is believed La Fontaine drew largely on the collections of Aesop's fables that were available in the seventeenth century (Huck, Hepler, & Hickman, 1987).

Modern-Day Fabulists

Modern-day fabulists include several well-known authors. Worthy of mention are Leo Lionni's *Frederick's Fables: A Leo Lionni Treasury of Favorite Stories* (1985), Arnold Lobel's *Fables* (1980), and Eric Carle's *Treasury of Classic Stories for Children: by Aesop, Hans Christian Andersen, and The Brothers Grimm* (1988). The trend in most of the books published today is not to state the moral at the end of the story; instead, it is left open for interpretation by the audience. This is especially true for authors who have taken fables and transformed them in some way by changing the characters, setting, or key events. In these cases, the moral of the story is rarely stated at the tale's conclusion.

What Are the Characteristics of Fables?

The characteristics of fables include the following elements:

■ Short, often less than a page long, involving only one event
■ Little development in the story setting
■ Animal characters with one dominant trait
■ Connection among conflict, action, and moral

Summary

Sutherland (1997) describes fables as brief narratives that take abstract ideas of behavior attempting to make them concrete and striking enough to be understood and remembered. The fable usually revolves around one event with little to no development or elaboration in the story setting. The characters are most often animals having one dominant trait (e.g., greed) involved in a situation where the reader is led to establishing a connection between the conflict, action, and moral found within the fable.

Reading Fables: What Are Examples of Each Characteristic from Actual Fables?

In this section, each characteristic will be discussed, books will be highlighted that illustrate the characteristic, and a sample lesson idea will be presented as a means of helping your students to expand their knowledge and comprehension of the fable.

CHARACTERISTIC: SHORT, OFTEN LESS THAN A PAGE LONG, INVOLVING ONLY ONE EVENT

Most fables are one to two paragraphs long and are found on a single page. For younger children, there are also fables in a picture book format by authors such as Leo Lionni and Brian Wildsmith.

"The Wolf and the Lamb," found in *Eric Carle's Treasury of Classic Stories for Children,* tells how a lamb outwits a wolf. The wolf informs the lamb, "I am hungry. I am going to eat you up." The lamb pleas for one last wish, and the wolf agrees to play music for her. The unfamiliar music prompts the shepherd to investigate the noise coming from his herd, and the lamb's life is saved when the shepherd discovers the wolf, hits him over the head with a big stick, and chases him away.

The Hare and the Tortoise, illustrated by Brian Wildsmith, revolves on a race between a hare and a tortoise to determine which of them is the fastest. The hare thought he was much more clever than the tortoise, and he felt sure he could win the race, since the tortoise had to also carry his house on his back. Distractions along the way prove to be the hare's undoing, as the slow but steady way of the tortoise make him the winner instead of the quick and careless hare.

One of Arnold Lobel's own fables, "King Lion and the Beetle," from his book *Fables,* shares how "it is the high and mighty who have the longest distance to fall." In this story, King Lion has an exalted opinion of himself. He decides to show his devoted subjects that their leader "is every inch a king." When he passes a tiny beetle, King Lion commands the beetle to bow. The beetle assures King Lion he is indeed bowing, and as the king peers more closely to the ground to see the bow, King Lion loses his balances, falls on his head, and rolls into a ditch covering himself in mud.

FOCUS ACTIVITY: OFTEN SHORT, INVOLVING ONLY ONE EVENT

■ Characteristic: Short, often less than a page long, usually involving only one event
■ Activity: Comic strips
■ Summary: Students will use a three- or four-frame comic strip to illustrate what happens in the story.
■ Materials: Copies of different fables, setting map, two copies of a comic strip frame, construction paper, markers or crayons, pencils, Reproducible 4.1 (Events in Action), Reproducible 4.2 (Comic Strip Template)

How Do You Do It?

Tell the students that they will examine different fables to identify the major event that is represented in each one. The purpose of the activity is to be able to recognize the key event, as well as the key actions that represent it in the narrative. After they have had practice doing this, the children may select a fable, identify the key event and actions, then write and illustrate it in a comic strip format.

Using several different fables, work with the students to identify the major event(s) of each one. The chart shown in Figure 4.1 is helpful in organizing

FIGURE 4.1 Highlighting a Fable's Key Event with a Short Summary

FABLE	KEY EVENT	SUMMARY
"The Fox and the Grapes"	Fox is trying to get the grapes hanging over his head just out of reach.	1. Fox goes for a walk. 2. He sees the grapes and tries to pull a bunch from the vine by stretching himself tall. 3. Fox leaps up and snaps at the grapes. 4. Fox leaves the vineyard.
"The Cocks and the Hens"	Two roosters fight over the hens in the farmyard.	1. Two cocks fight in the farmyard. 2. The winner flies to a rooftop to crow about his victory, while the loser retreats to a corner of the yard. 3. An eagle swoops down and seizes the cock on the rooftop. 4. The other cock, seeing his rival gone, takes his place with the hens.

this information by fable, key event, and short summary; Reproducible 4.1 is a variation of such a chart. By doing this part of the activity together, the students see how to identify the key event of the fable, and then they summarize briefly the actions that illustrate the key event. The examples used in Figure 4.1 were taken from *The Fables of Aesop,* retold by Frances Barnes-Murphy.

After the students have had practice identifying the events and major actions to illustrate for several different fables, then, as a class, select one fable to illustrate in a comic strip format. Before actually illustrating the fable, first hand out copies of different comic strip pages for the children to critique. Ask them to focus on the different ways the comic strips are organized. For example:

- The number of frames (i.e., 1, 2, 3, or 4)
- How the dialogue is written and positioned (i.e., bubbles, drawn out to the side with a line)
- How the setting is established (i.e., in a box drawn at the left or right side, at the top, or at the bottom of the strip)
- Clues given by the character's expressions and gestures (i.e., big eyes, arms crossed)
- How some actions are emphasized more than others (i.e., POW! WHAM!)

This information can be organized into a chart format (see Figure 4.2) to help the students remember the guidelines to follow when they eventually create their own comic strip.

As a class, illustrate one of the fables. Different groups can each take an action to illustrate on a piece of construction paper. For example, one frame might be the fox going for a walk, the next would be the fox stretching tall to reach the grapes, the third would be the fox jumping and snapping at the grapes, and the last would be the fox walking away in disgust. When all groups are done, the different papers, or "frames," can be brought together in the correct sequence to illustrate the fable (see Reproducible 4.2).

After the students have had practice in identifying and organizing the key event and actions of the fable into a comic strip format, then let them work alone or with a partner to do the same activity with a fable of their choice. Remember, it will take them some time to select the fable they wish to work with, so be sure to allow the students adequate time. As they decide which fable to select, they are reading and critiquing many fables before deciding on the per-

FIGURE 4.2   Guidelines for Comic Strip Format

Number of frames	■ One ■ Two ■ Three ■ Four
How dialogue is written	■ Bubbles ■ Drawn out to the side with a line ■ Written in a box

fect one. Once this has been accomplished, then let the students use Reproducible 4.1 (Events in Action) to identify the key event and actions that reflect it. Once they have done this, then encourage them to draft preliminary plans for their strip by using the "Draft of Illustration" portion shown on the reproducible master. Remind them it is only a draft of their ideas, and that detail work should be saved for the actual strip itself. Some students may choose to jot down ideas for their illustration as opposed to the actual rough sketch of their picture.

Extensions
1. The student's comic strips can be cut into four parts, placed in a folder, and used as a center activity to practice sequencing skills.
2. Students can use their critical thinking skills to match the comic strip with the appropriate moral or lesson. It could be organized into a bulletin board format or as a center activity.

Note: Two to three days will be needed:

Day One involves the class working as a group to identify the fable's key event and actions that support it, and then working in groups to create frames for their comic strip.

Day Two and possibly Day Three allow the students to select their own fable, identify the event/actions, and create a comic strip to illustrate their fable.

Reproducible masters 4.1 and 4.2 may be found at the end of this chapter.

CHARACTERISTIC: LITTLE DEVELOPMENT IN THE STORY SETTING

The shortness of each fable is testimony to this characteristic, since it is difficult to have much development of anything when the stories are only a couple of paragraphs in length. The text gives brief reference to a setting through random placement of phrases, as in Arnold Lobel's "The Ducks and the Fox" *(Fables):* "Two duck sisters were waddling down the road to the pond for their morning swim" or "The two ducks waddled down the same road to the pond."

Heidi Holder's *Aesop's Fables* includes "The Country Mouse and the City Mouse." The setting in this story is established by the "city" and "country" connection to each mouse. City Mouse goes first to visit Country Mouse, thus establishing the major setting for the story. This is reinforced by City Mouse's questions to Country Mouse regarding the dullness of her life "with nothing but woods and meadows, mountains and brooks" around her. City Mouse convinces Country Mouse to visit the city to listen to "conversations of the world instead of the chirping of birds." The shift into the city develops the setting a bit more than the country. There are references to couches of crimson velvet, rich Persian carpet, and ivory carvings. A noisy party and barking dogs force the mice to flee in terror to a corner of the room. Country Mouse decides the trappings of the city are not enough to keep her from appreciating peace and quiet of her country home to the fear and danger of the City.

The Fables of Aesop, retold and illustrated by Frances Barnes-Murphy, includes the fable "The Crow and the Pitcher." The story focuses on a thirsty crow and his persistence in finding a means to satisfy his thirst. To solve his problem, he methodically drops pebbles into a pitcher to make the water rise to within his reach. The setting for this story is simply the pitcher and the pebbles used by the crow to get to the water.

"The King of the Barnyard" in *Androcles and the Lion and Other Aesop Fables,* retold in verse by Tom Paxton, is another example of how little the setting of the story is developed. It is first established through the title "King of the Barnyard." Two other references in the fable, hen house and fence post, help to confirm the barnyard as where the story takes place.

FOCUS ACTIVITY: LITTLE DEVELOPMENT IN THE STORY SETTING

- ▪ Characteristic: Little development in the story setting
- ▪ Activity: Setting map
- ▪ Summary: The setting map helps students determine that there is a lack of references to the setting for the fable.
- ▪ Materials: Fable, Reproducible 4.3 (Graphic Organizer for Fables Containing One Setting), Reproducible 4.4 (Graphic Organizer for Fables Containing Two Settings), Reproducible 4.5 (Fable Story Map)

How Do You Do It?

Note: This is a simple, quick activity to heighten students' awareness toward the lack of development for the setting of the story. It is important to keep in mind that setting is but one of the literary elements found within most narratives. But, it is also important for the students to recognize that, relative to the fable, there are few references regarding where the story takes place.

Select a fable to read aloud and critique with the students. Before reading, ask them to listen for references that are made in the story regarding the setting. After reading, ask the students to share the hints or clues they heard. Determine if there is one setting for the story or more than one setting. For example, in the case of "The Country Mouse and the City Mouse" found in Heidi Holder's *Aesop's Fables,* there would be two settings: the Country Mouse's home and the City Mouse's home. Show the students how to jot down the references to each setting on the setting map (Figure 4.3).

Once the students have had practice in selecting key elements of the setting, they can then read another fable on their own to identify the setting attributes in their response logs. They may insert a photocopy of the graphic organizer or draw the graphic themselves. Another variation to identifying elements of the setting is to combine the lesson on recognition of a major event with key actions. Reproducibles 4.3, 4.4, and 4.5 may be used for this purpose.

The story map in Reproducible 4.5 ties in the references to the setting as each relates to the key actions taken in the story. In some cases, there may not be setting changes of any significance. Remember, it is important not to overkill the concept of setting in this lesson. The idea is to help students see that there is very little development of setting in a fable. This particular lesson is designed to be a quick and easy mini-lesson to reinforce this idea. Some students will find the graphic organizer helpful in pulling out this information, whereas other students will not need it at all.

Extensions

1. The students can compare the illustration and text to determine what reveals more information regarding the setting of the story. In some cases, the illustrator has provided many clues that are not included in the text.

FIGURE 4.3 Map Highlighting Key Element of the Setting Found in the Fable

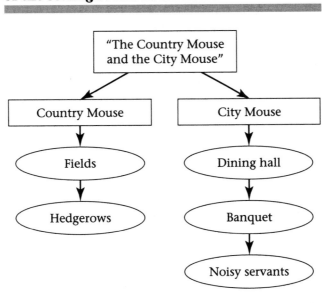

2. As an art project, ask students to provide their own illustrations for different fables. These illustrations can then be used as a game or center activity where the students match up the fable with the most appropriate illustration. Students must use their critical thinking skills to do this as they listen or read each fable to determine the illustration that matches it.
3. Compare and contrast a picture book or chapter in a novel with a fable to see how the setting is developed in each.

Note: This activity is designed to be a quick 10- to 15-minute mini-lesson. Students needing additional reinforcement regarding this concept can be pulled to the side as a small group or worked with one-on-one in a teacher/student conference session.

Reproducible masters 4.3, 4.4, and 4.5 may be found at the end of this chapter.

CHARACTERISTIC: ANIMAL CHARACTERS WITH ONE DOMINANT TRAIT

The third characteristic of fables pertains to the fact that the characters associated with fables are usually animals and one-dimensional. These two characteristics are addressed jointly in the lesson following this discussion.

The Characters Are Usually Animals

The characters in fables are diverse, ranging from grasshoppers and ants to ducks and a fox to a tadpole and a minnow. Of course, there are always exceptions, but, for the most part, the characters usually are animals.

A retelling of a well-known fable, "The Grasshopper and the Ants," is found in *Eric Carle's Treasury of Classic Stories for Children*. The whole story revolves on how the ants work hard all summer long to gather and store their food, while the grasshopper plays his fiddle and sings songs. When winter arrives, the hungry grasshopper is turned away by all but one family of ants who invite him in to provide entertainment in exchange for food.

"The Lion and the Mouse" is an Aesop fable included in *Aesop's Fables* by Michael Hague. The classic story shares how the life of a mouse is spared by a lion who is amused by the mouse's promise to someday return the favor. Soon after this encounter, the mouse gets his chance to save the life of the lion when the lion becomes ensnared by a hunter's ropes.

"The Tiger's Tale" is included in *The Dragon's Tale and Other Animal Fables of the Zodiac,* retold and illustrated by Demi. In this story, Fox outwits Tiger by convincing him the Heavenly Dragon has appointed Fox king of all the animals. Fox leads Tiger to a clearing, where all the animals flee upon seeing them. Fox then commands Tiger to leave his kingdom, and Tiger, not realizing the animals are afraid of him, not the fox, scurries away.

Richard and Judy Dockrey Young include the animal fable "How Br'er Rabbit Outsmarted the Frogs" in their book *African-American Folktales for Young Readers*. The major characters in this story are Br'er Rabbit, Br'er 'Coon, and the frogs living in the river. The frogs develop a plan to outsmart Br'er 'Coon, so that he would not be able to catch and take the frogs home as his dinner. The bullfrogs call out, "Here he comes," and the little frogs peep, "Here he comes," as a warning to all the frogs of the river that Br'er 'Coon is nearby. Br'er Rabbit develops a plan to help his friend Br'er 'Coon by tricking the frogs into digging a grave for the recently departed Br'er 'Coon. When the grave is deep enough that the frogs cannot jump out, Rabbit tells Coon to arise and pick up his groceries, since the frogs cannot get away. Br'er 'Coon ends up with enough frogs to feed him and his family for many years.

The Characters Are One-Dimensional

In most other stories, the literary elements of characters are fully developed in that they have many character traits. The characters, in these cases, are called round characters, and readers are able to discern much about them through how they look, act, speak, or think. In contrast to this are the flat, one-dimensional characters found in fables. The animals representing these characters stand for such simple traits as being honest, clever, stupid, sly, or wise, and their actions in the story are connected to these same traits. This connection between the animals and their traits also serves as a means of presenting the conflict for the narrative.

Susan Lowell's retelling of the tortoise and the hare story is entitled *Tortoise and the Jackrabbit*. Her version adds a southwestern flair by bringing in animals and scenery native to that region. The cocky Jackrabbit and the persistent Tortoise, both confident in their own way, embark on a race to determine which of them is faster. After the first couple of pages, the reader is pulling for the Tortoise to win. The cocky and boastful Hare simply begs for a comeuppance, and true to the story, the Tortoise does win. Stopping along the way for a nibble and a nap, the Hare is left behind as the patient and persistent Tortoise crosses the finish line first.

Eric Carle's version of "The Fox and the Crow" is found in his book *Eric Carle's Treasury of Classic Stories for Children*. In this fable, clever and wily Fox outwits vain Crow to get the food Crow had been holding in his beak for Fox's hungry son. Through use of flattery, Fox uses a loud voice to exclaim at Crow's beauty and talent. Preening Crow drops his food in order to sing for Fox and her son, and Fox takes the food for her son's lunch. They then move away as Fox tells her son, "Let's move away from here. I find the crow's song so irritating." Thus, sly Fox uses Crow's vanity to outwit him.

The Fables of Aesop, retold by Frances Barnes-Murphy, contains the fable "The Fox, The Wolf, and the Moon Cheese." Fox is convinced a large, round, yellow cheese is at the bottom of a well, so he jumps into a bucket to lower himself down to get it. He soon discovers his "cheese" is nothing more than the moon's reflection. His cleverness in getting to the bottom of the well is surpassed by his stupidity in not thinking of a way to return to the top. When a greedy, hungry wolf goes by, Fox tricks the wolf into getting into the other bucket. The weight of Wolf makes Fox's bucket shoot to the top, freeing him from the well, but now leaving gullible Wolf at the bottom with nothing more than the moon's reflection as company.

FOCUS ACTIVITY: ANIMAL CHARACTERS WITH ONE DOMINANT TRAIT

- ■ Characteristic: Animal characters with one dominant trait
- ■ Activity: Character analysis
- ■ Summary: Characters will be analyzed to determine the traits that represent them.
- ■ Materials: Fables, Reproducible 4.6 (Character Trait Analysis)

How Do You Do It?

Give groups of students two or three fables to read through and analyze at the beginning of class. Ask them to make notes concerning the characters in each one, and then to present their notes to the rest of the class. After the students have had enough time to do this, then meet back as a large group and share information. Make an informal list on an overhead or the chalkboard as each group reports its information. Students should be able to determine that the majority of characters are usually animals in the fables.

Select one fable to read aloud with the students. After reading, identify the characters. For example, using Susan Lowell's *Tortoise and the Jackrabbit,* write down the major characters of the story on the board (see Figure 4.4).

Next, ask the students to reread the fable to determine words to describe the characters in the story (see Figure 4.5). Tell them these words are called *traits*—distinguishing qualities of the character. After students have determined words to describe the characters in the story, then ask what behaviors in the story illustrate each of these traits (see Figure 4.6).

After discussing several traits that describe each character, ask students to consider how the animals representing these characters stand for such simple traits as honest or dishonest, clever or stupid, or foolish or wise. When considering this, ask where they see Tortoise and Jackrabbit. A class chart could be started to keep track of the different kinds of characters that are represented in each fable (see Figure 4.7). This chart would be useful later if the students decide to write their own fable.

FIGURE 4.4   Identifying Major Characters Found in the Fable

FIGURE 4.5   Rereading Story to Determine Descriptive Words about the Character

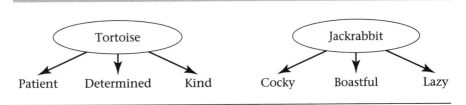

FIGURE 4.6 Identifying Key Behaviors That Illustrate the Descriptive Word for the Character

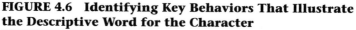

Tortoise → Patient, Determined, Kind

Patient → Tortoise listened patiently to Jackrabbit's boast that he was the fastest.

Jackrabbit → Cocky, Boastful, Lazy

Cocky → Jackrabbit claimed that he was the fastest runner in the desert, and that he would win the race between them.

FIGURE 4.7 Class Chart to Track Types of Characters and the Traits That Are Associated with Them

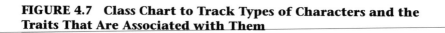

FABLE	CHARACTER	TRAIT
"The Fox and the Crow"	Fox	Sly
	Crow	Gullible, vain

Once students have had practice in the large group with character trait analysis, and they understand what is meant by *trait,* then let them work alone or with a partner to do the activity. This can be done on a formal graphic organizer (see Reproducible 4.6) or simply jotted down in their response logs to share in the teacher/student conference session.

Extensions
1. The students can keep adding on to the class character trait chart (Figure 4.7).
2. Compare how the same animal is depicted in different fables (e.g., the ants and grasshopper in "The Grasshopper and the Ants" and "The Ant and the Grasshopper").

Note: This activity could be spread across two to three days:

Day One is the analysis of the fables to determine that animals are represented much more than people. The students would need time to examine different fables, and then meet back as a class to share findings and draw conclusions (characters in fables are usually animals).

Day Two involves the students identifying particular traits for each character and the behavior that illustrates each trait. The class chart could be begun at this time.

Day Three allows the students to work on the assignment independently and meet back as a group to share their findings. This information could be written on the class chart by the students.

Reproducible master 4.6 may be found at the end of this chapter.

CHARACTERISTIC: CONNECTION AMONG CONFLICT, ACTION, AND MORAL

The conflict in the fable is between the characters. Their actions related to this conflict illustrate the moral (representing the theme of the story), and this moral again connects back to the conflict found within the narrative. For example, the conflict between the Tortoise and the Hare over who is the fastest illustrates that "slow and steady wins the race." Other stories illustrate how it is possible to have too much of a good thing; knowledge will not always take the place of simple observation; or how no act of kindness, no matter how small, is ever wasted. These morals are either stated at the end or implied within the story itself.

It's Mine, a fable by Leo Lionni, tells the story of three quarrelsome frogs: Milton, Rupert, and Lydia. The three frogs are so busy arguing over who the water, the earth, and the air belong to that they never begin to appreciate the beauty and peace around them, much less each other. When their home is flooded, they share their hopes and fears as they are forced to seek shelter on a single rock surrounded by water. When the water clears, the frogs have learned to appreciate their world and each other, and how they can share it all together.

Demi's "The Ox's Tale," in *The Dragon's Tale and Other Animal Fables of the Chinese Zodiac,* tells how tigers outwit some oxen grazing in a field. The tigers knew they would stand a chance if the oxen remained together, so the tigers devised a plan to sow distrust among the oxen. The tigers whispered evil stories and gossip of one ox against the other. Birds flew to the oxen, landed on their backs, and repeated the tigers' evil stories and gossip. The oxen soon began to distrust each other, quarreling and charging at each other, and, in some cases, grazing apart from the rest. "The quarrels of friends are the opportunities of foes" the fable states. The tigers knew they would be soon eating very well, since the scattered oxen would make an easy meal of them all.

Heidi Holder's *Aesop's Fables* contains the fable "The Fox and the Grapes." In this narrative, a hungry fox tries numerous times to obtain a bunch of grapes, all to no avail. After many jumps, the weary and hungry fox turns away. As he leaves, he mutters to himself that the grapes are sour. His reaction to his failure to get the grapes serves as an illustration for the moral: "There are those who pretend to despise what they cannot obtain."

John Bierhorst's *Doctor Coyote: A Native American Aesop's Fables* is a collection of stories about Coyote, who travels from place to place as he tries to outsmart everyone else while often outsmarting himself. The moral for each story is shown in italicized text at the end, and each illustrates how Coyote becomes a little bit wiser as the result of his adventures.

FOCUS ACTIVITY: CONFLICT, CHARACTER ACTIONS, AND MORAL

- ▩ Characteristic: Connection among conflict, action, and moral
- ▩ Activity: Puppet theater
- ▩ Summary: A puppet theater will be made so that students can use the characters to act out the conflict and underlying moral of the story.
- ▩ Materials: Fable of choice, construction paper or tagboard, stapler, plastic bag (optional), Popsicle sticks (optional), markers or colors, Reproducible 4.7 (Puppet Theater Story Board Notes)

How Do You Do It?

Explain to the students that they will make a mini-puppet theater to use as a means of retelling a fable. They will have to make the characters and create the setting, so this draws in concepts learned in the previous characteristics about fables. Review characters and setting before reading a fable to the students, and discuss how the development of the characters and setting in fables differs from those in other types of genres (e.g., mysteries).

Read a fable to the students. After reading, identify the character and setting. Using *It's Mine* by Leo Lionni, this information would be reflected in Figure 4.8. (A variation of Figure 4.8 is shown in Reproducible 4.7.)

Using two pieces of 6" × 4" squares of construction paper, tear or cut each character out. A third piece could be used to represent the toad, and the scraps may be used to decorate their setting. Take the piece of construction paper or tagboard, fold in half from left to right, and turn up the bottom by about an inch. Staple the left and right side of the paper (see X in Figure 4.9) to hold the fold in place. This is where the students can position the characters as they retell the story.

The setting for the story may be drawn on the puppet theater (big piece of construction paper). On one side, draw the island in the middle of Rainbow Pond, and on the other side, the flooded island could be drawn. A plastic bag could be clipped or stapled to the back of the theater to hold the story characters when they are not being used.

FIGURE 4.8   Preparing to Make a Puppet Theater by Determining Characters, Setting, Major Events, and Key Actions

CHARACTER	SETTING	MAJOR EVENT	KEY ACTIONS
Milton	Island	Three frogs constantly argue over who the earth, water, and air belong to between them.	On an island in the middle of Rainbow Pond, three frogs argue over who owns the earth, water, and air.
Rupert	Flooded island		The frogs huddle together on a single rock when their island floods.
Lydia	Island		The waters subside, and the frogs rejoice in the peace and beauty around them, and how much they appreciate each other.

FIGURE 4.9   Folding Construction Paper in Half from Left to Right, and Turning Up the Bottom by about One Inch

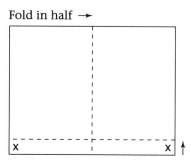

Turn up bottom by one inch and staple the left and right sides to hold in place.

Use the puppet theater and characters to briefly retell the story with the students. Brainstorm with the students possible messages the author is trying to impart through his story. Be sure to ask students to tell what it was in the story that made them think of a particular message.

Once the process for making the puppet theater is complete, then let the students select their own fable and make a puppet theater for it. Ask them to write two or three different possible morals on an index card or piece of paper, and when they present their fable to the rest of the class, the class could identify the most appropriate moral from the selection of choices.

Extensions

1. The students can take their puppet theaters to a younger grade level to share with other students.

2. The students can compare different versions of the same fable, and compare how the moral is written in each one. For example, in *Aesop's Fables* by Heidi Holder, the moral for "The Hare and the Tortoise" is "Perseverance and determination compensate for the absence of natural gifts." In contrast to this is the moral embedded in Brian Wildsmith's version of the same story. In the last sentence of the text, it says, "All the animals gathered round the tortoise while he told how, in his slow and steady way, he had won the race from the quick and careless hare." Another example is the many different versions of "The Country Mouse and the City Mouse" that are available.

3. Throughout the year, occasionally read a fable and ask the students to try to figure out what the moral would be for the story. In some cases, it might be wise to offer a few from which to select, but be sure the students explain why they chose a particular moral over another.

4. The students' finished products can be organized into an interactive bulletin board. The puppet theaters with the characters can be placed in the middle of the bulletin board, with the morals written on strips of paper tacked out to the side. The students can take turns determining which moral goes with each fable.

Note: This activity can be accomplished in two to three days:

Day One serves as a review of characters, setting, major event, and key actions in relationship to fables. Model how to make the puppet theater, and retell the story with the students.

Day Two is for the students to select their own fable and construct their puppet theater and characters. If time permits, they can practice retelling the story.

Day Three allows the students to share their puppet theaters with the rest of the class. The students will have fun trying to figure out which moral is the correct choice for each one.

Reproducible master 4.7 may be found at the end of this chapter.

WRITING YOUR OWN FABLES

Figure 4.10 lists the activities used to illustrate the stages of writing and the recursive nature of the process that are included in this section. As students prepare to write during the prewriting stage, a storyboard organizer will help them get a rough sketch of their ideas. Once they have begun to write, they

FIGURE 4.10 Writing Stages with Corresponding Activities Related to Fables

WRITING STAGE	ACTIVITY
Prewriting	(1) Storyboard
Drafting	(2) Writing the fable
Conferencing for Content	(3) Checklist
→Revising	→Making changes
Conferencing for Conventions	(4) CUPS Check
→Revising	→Making changes
Publishing	(5) Sharing

can use the checklist as a guideline to ensure they are including key elements of the fable. The checklist is helpful when conferencing with a peer or with the teacher. The focus in conferencing for conventions is on the CUPS technique, where the students can serve as peer editors to focus on aspects on *capitalization, usage, punctuation,* and *spelling.*

FOCUS ACTIVITY: BECOMING A FABULIST

■ Activity: Writing fables in comic strip format
■ Summary: Students will make plans for their own fable using the characteristics of fables to guide them. The fable will be organized into a comic strip format to encourage the use of brevity. However, once completed, students can then use the comic strip as an outline to write it in a narrative format.
■ Materials: Markers or colors, Reproducible 4.2 (Comic Strip Template), Reproducible 4.8 (Storyboard Organizer for Comic Strip)

How Do You Do It?

The first part of this activity is prewriting.

STAGE OF THE WRITING PROCESS

Prewriting   ■ Reviewing comic strip format
            ■ Choosing story elements
            ■ Organizing the storyboard

Review with the students the format followed when they analyzed an existing fable and rewrote it in a comic strip format. They can follow this same procedure to write their own original fable. Refer again to the first characteristic (short, involving only one event) discussed earlier in this chapter, and the section on analyzing the major event and key actions that represent it.

Students need to have in mind a particular message they want to communicate to their audience prior to writing their fable. Since the purpose of fables is to teach or inform, then the fable the students write should tie back in to the moral of the story. Students may feel more comfortable working with a partner for this project, because trying to relate the moral to a particular story can be difficult to do.

After the students have selected the message (moral), they can begin to make decisions regarding what the major event will be in their fable. Once these decisions have been made, then it is simply a matter of planning the actions and the characters that best represent the event/actions. Here is an example:

1. I have selected the message: "There are those who pretend to despise what they cannot obtain."
2. Two contestants compete in a baking contest.
3. Key actions to represent this:
   ▦ The contestants are standing beside their baked food.
   ▦ The judge samples the food of the first contestant.
   ▦ The judge samples the food of the second contestant.
   ▦ The second contestant is declared the winner, and the first contestant says she did not really want to win anyway.
4. Animals in the story:
   ▦ First contestant—Crow
   ▦ Second contestant—Hen

Students can also use the transformation technique discussed in Chapter 3 on folktales. Also, the students can use the storyboard shown in Reproducible Figure 4.8 to help organize their information for their fable.

STAGE OF THE WRITING PROCESS

Drafting   ▦ Writing dialogue and using stick figures
              ▦ Writing the strip

Once the students have made preliminary plans for writing, they are ready to begin the actual writing of the fable using the graphic organizer as a support guide as they work. The graphic organizer will serve as a reminder of the key characteristics for fables. The comic strip template (Reproducible 4.2) can be used, and students can draw in dialogue boxes with stick figures (see Figure 4.11).

Another option is to write the dialogue on paper, before trying to organize into the comic strip. Here is an example:

Box 1:	Hen:	My vegetable soup is almost done. I hope the judges like it.
	Crow:	I have been working all day on my sugar cake. The judges are going to love it.
Box 2:	Judge:	Hmmmmm . . . Some mighty fine smells, ladies. Slurp, slurp. Nibble, nibble.
Box 3:	Judge:	I declare Mrs. Hen the winner. Never have I tasted soup so delicious.

FIGURE 4.11   Using Stick Figures to Draft Cartoon Strip

Box 4: Hen: Oh, thank you, Judge.

Crow: What a stupid contest. I only entered so I would have something to do today. I don't care about that fat old bird winning.

Mini-Lesson

Take a fable the class is familiar with and write dialogue for it using the stick figures or the boxes. Show students how to add in the appropriate punctuation (added text is shown by bold print).

> **The** Hen **whispered quietly,** *"My vegetable soup is almost done. I hope the judges like it."*

> **The** Crow **said, using a smug voice,** *"I have been working all day on my sugar cake. The judges are going to love it."*

STAGE OF THE WRITING PROCESS

Conferencing for Content ▨ Using a checklist for self and for peer conference

When students are ready to review their first draft of the comic strip with someone else, they can either conference with a peer, a group of peers, the class, or the teacher. A checklist format works well when doing this. The student needs to read through the fable one time with everyone listening first, then reread the fable several more times, with other members of the conference group taking notes or asking questions. Members of the group may decide to focus on one element for the writer (e.g., message). This is one reason why the checklist format works well, since sometimes it is hard for students to think of questions to ask. The elements included on the checklist can be used as a guide for questions they would like answered. The checklist shown in Figure 4.12 has been adapted for use with fables.

Mini-Lesson

Before asking the students to conference, invite them to join you as a large group. Read a fable that you have been working on, and ask them to give you feedback using the checklist as a guide. Encourage them to ask questions that are not on the checklist, but, nevertheless, are questions they had concerning your story while it was being read. This lays the groundwork for the students to successfully conference with each other.

FIGURE 4.12 Conferencing Checklist for Fables

POINTS TO PONDER...	NOTES...
1. Message of the story	
2. Major event	
3. Key actions	
4. Characters	
5. Setting clues	
6. Story sense	

The elements in the checklist are framed in phrases to guide the listener (or help the listener focus) as the reader shares the fable, as in the following:

1. *Message:* What is the moral of the story? What is the story trying to teach the listener?
2. *Major Event:* On what event does the story revolve?
3. *Key Actions:* Do the actions present in the story adequately reflect the major event?
4. *Characters:* How are the characters represented in the story? Do their character traits help reflect what the fable is trying to communicate?
5. *Setting:* What clues are given in the story regarding the setting?
6. *Story Sense:* Does the story make sense? Does it flow from one action to the next to reflect the major event?

These questions can be posted in the conference corner as an additional reference tool for the students. This process is effective for the reader and the listener, since these same elements should be apparent in their own fable. By listening to the reader, each student is having to critically examine the fable to determine if it contains the characteristics that make it a fable.

The students can use the checklists filled out by their conference partners, as well as the oral feedback they received, to make adjustments and revisions to the first draft of their comic strip/fable.

Mini-Lesson

A good mini-lesson at this time is to take the same fable you used to model how to conference, and work with the students to incorporate feedback that was received back into the fable. Help them understand that it is not necessary to use all the suggestions that were given, but to use enough to make improvements to the fable.

STAGE OF THE WRITING PROCESS

Revising   ■   Using feedback from the conference to make changes

After students have made content revisions, and they have had these improvements affirmed by a peer, group, or teacher, then they are ready to proceed to the next stage of conferencing that focuses on the capitalization, usage, punctuation, and spelling aspects of their writing. For others to read and check their paper, it is necessary that the paper be legible. In some cases, students may need to rewrite their paper to assure this. They will catch some, but not all, of their grammar mistakes when they do. As they write words they are not sure about, they can underline them lightly as a reminder to go back and check for correct spelling.

STAGE OF THE WRITING PROCESS

Conferencing for Conventions   ■   Doing a CUPS check

In either the peer-editing session or the teacher-editing session, the draft of the student's paper gets a CUPS check. Notations (Capitalization, Usage, Punctuation, and Spelling) are made next to the mistake or directly beside the line that has the error. The student goes back to find the mistake and make the correction on his or her own. Here is an example:

C, S   the night held his shield high.

The corrections that need to be made include the capital at the beginning of the sentence, and the spelling of *night* should be changed to *knight.* The sentence should read:

The knight held his shield high.

The student would know that there were errors somewhere in that line, since the errors were indicated directly to the left of the line. This technique becomes a way for students to become accountable for their own errors. Instead of having someone make the correction for them, the error is noted or indicated on the line, and they must go back to determine what needs to be corrected.

Mini-Lesson

Model how to use the CUPS technique with a piece of writing. Show how to indicate errors have been made by making notations to the left of the line. Then show how to make corrections by using the notations at the left of the line as a guide.

After students have finished examining their drafts for convention errors, they need to be sure they follow through and make the corrections. They can rewrite the comic strip, if necessary, and then meet with the teacher as a final quality checkpoint. Once this has been done, the students can make a formal draft of their comic strip. However, some students may prefer to make their own. Once they are done, they can mount the individual boxes of their comic strip on construction paper or tagboard.

STAGE OF THE WRITING PROCESS

Publishing ▨ Sharing
▨ Combining class strips into a comics page

The students who participated in this project could make photo copies of their strips and combine them into a comic strip page. The strips could also be organized into a bulletin board in the class or in the school. Other students could be challenged to match the moral with the appropriate comic strip.

Note: This lesson could last up to two school weeks or longer. It is dependent on the amount of time the students have to work on the project.

Days One through Two involves the students making decisions regarding the message, event, key actions, characters, and setting.

Days Three through Four permit the students to work on the first draft of their comic strip.

Day Five and possibly Day Six allow students to conference for content and make necessary revisions. In some cases, it may be necessary to extend this another day. It is dependent on the amount of work needed to make improvements.

Days Seven and Eight allow students to conference for conventions and make necessary revisions. They can begin work on a formal draft.

Day Nine requires students need to receive a final go-ahead from the teacher before deciding on how to formally publish their project.

Day Ten involves a time for all students to share with the others in the class.

Reproducible master 4.8 may be found at the end of this chapter.

Tieing in to Technology

INTERNET CONNECTIONS

Internet sites that contain links to the text versions of fables include the following:

- ▩ http://www.pacificnet.net/~johnr/aesop/aesop1.html
  Contains an index of many different fables with moral listed alongside. In some cases, an audio version is available.
- ▩ http://www.etext.lib.virginia.edu/cgibin/t...ng&data=.kvk.
  Arcguve.ebg-parsed&part=0
  This archive has links to over 200 fables.

Students can visit these sites to access hundreds of different fables for the classroom library. They can read the fables then work together to determine the moral, brainstorm modern-day versions along with a modern-day wording of the moral, and work to develop illustrations that represent major elements of the fable.

PRESENTATIONS

Freelance Graphics (Lotus) and *Powerpoint* (Microsoft) are two programs that students can use to create a presentation of information they would like to share. Students can provide a summary of a particular story they have read, highlight a genre by using various stories to illustrate all of the characteristics, analyze one characteristic of a genre by using different stories (e.g., a strong sense of magic found in folktales), or add text and graphics to create an electronic version of their own original or transformations of stories.

Using the same ideas discussed in Writing Your Own Fables (Chapter 3), the students can access different graphics and input text to create their comic strip. Once printed out, the students have the frames ready to connect together. The same graphics used to analyze the characteristics discussed concerning fables can be saved as templates. For example, in Reproducible 4.5, the students create a story map for a fable they have read. To do this activity, the students can open the "template" file and then type their text into the appropriate place on the graphic organizer (i.e., Title of Fable, Major Event, Action, and Setting Clues). Be sure to remind students to save their file under a different name so that the template is not written over with the new information they have added. Many of the word-processing programs have the table/chart format that can be used to create templates, too. Figure 4.1 is such an example of a chart created with a word-processing program. In this case, the students could type in information pertaining to identifying the Fable, Key Event, and Summary.

MULTIMEDIA

Kid Pix Studio (Broderbund) is a multimedia paint and animation program where students can create productions combining animation, video, special effects, photos, music, and much more. They can choose from different projects to help depict fables they have read or they can create original versions of their fables:

- ▩ Moopies (moving pictures) help create animations.
- ▩ Stampinator is where action-packed adventures can be created using animated stamps as actors.

■ Digital Puppets are on-screen marionettes that are controlled by keys on the keyboard. Students select a puppet and sounds or music to accompany the puppet.

■ SlideShow links together as many as 99 "moving vans" loaded with pictures, animations, and digital movies. Sound effects can also be added.

■ Wacky TV contains 100 digital clips to which students can add special effects. They can also be pasted into a Kid Pix picture.

Annotated Bibliography: Fables

Barnes-Murphy, Frances. (1994). *The Fables of Aesop*. New York: Lowthrop, Lee & Shepard.

This is a collection of 103 Aesop's fables with a profile by the author on Aesop and his fables. The illustrations for the book, done by Rowan Barnes-Murphy, range from full-color paintings to pen-and-ink drawings. The fables are brief, one-paragraph narratives with an implied moral set within each one.

Bierhorst, John. (1987). *Doctor Coyote: A Native American Aesop's Fables*. New York: Macmillan.

This collection of tales brings together the fables of Aesop and the Native American coyote tales. Irrepressible Coyote, the softhearted trickster, grows a little wiser as the result of each adventure. The moral for each tale is shown at the end of the narrative in italicized text.

Brown, Marcia. (1961). *Once a Mouse . . . A Fable Cut in Wood*. New York: Macmillan.

A retelling of a fable from ancient India chronicles how an old hermit, mighty at magic, attempts to save the life of his little pet by changing the mouse to a stout cat, to a big dog, and finally, to a tiger. After the tiger lords it over the other animals in the forest, the old hermit cautions him not to put on airs, since he was once a "wretched little mouse." The disbelieving tiger decides to kill the old hermit, but instead the hermit turns the tiger back into "a frightened, humble, little mouse." The story ends with the old hermit contemplating the same thoughts about *big* and *little* he had pondered at the beginning of the story.

Carle, Eric. (1988). *Eric Carle's Treasury of Classic Stories for Children: By Aesop, Hans Christian Andersen and the Brothers Grimm*. New York: Orchard Books.

Eleven of Aesop's fables are included in Carle's book. One page of text is accompanied by one full-color illustration. In some stories, the moral is stated as the last lines of the text, but in others, the moral is implied within the story.

Demi. (1996). *The Dragon's Tale and Other Animal Fables of the Chinese Zodiac*. New York: Henry Holt.

This is a collection of stories involving the 12 animals of the Chinese zodiac. The stories are brief fables with color illustrations, and the morals are set off in red print at the end of the fable. Stories include tales about the Rat, Ox, Tiger, Rabbit, Dragon, Snake, Horse, Goat, Monkey, Rooster, Dog, and Boar.

Hague, Michael. (1985). *Aesop's Fables*. New York: Henry Holt.

This is a collection of the most familiar of Aesop's fables selected and illustrated by Hague. Among the stories included are "The Town Mouse and the Country Mouse," "The Lion and the Mouse," "The Fox and the Goat," "The Cat and the Birds," "The Crow and the Pitcher," "The Mice in Council," "The Marriage of the Sun," "The Hare and the Tortoise," "The Wolf and the Kid," "The Fox and the Grapes," "The Ass in the Lion's Skin," "The Fox and the Crow," and "The Cock and the Jewel."

Holder, Heidi. (1981). *Aesop's Fables*. New York: Viking Penguin.

Nine fables are illustrated by Holder, including "The Country Mouse and the City Mouse," "The Fox and the Grapes," and "The Hare and the Tortoise." The fables range from one page to three pages, and are accompanied by at least one full-page illustration. The moral is stated in italicized text at the end of the fable.

Lionni, Leo. (1967). *Frederick*. New York: Pantheon.

As his friends gather corn, berries, nuts, and straw for the winter, Frederick collects sun rays, colors, and words. Winter arrives, and the mice soon use up their stores of food. They turn to Frederick and ask him to share his supplies, upon which he warms their bodies with the sun rays, fills their minds with paintings, and shares his poetry from his stage. The story effectively illustrates how people rely on all of their talents in times of need.

Lionni, Leo. (1968). *The Biggest House in the World*. New York: Pantheon.

A young snail boasts that one day he will have the biggest house in the world. He is cautioned by his father, "Some things are better small." The father tells the snail a story of another snail who had also made such a wish. The snail had twisted and twitched, making his shell grow larger and larger with pointy bulges, bright colors, and beautiful designs. The father concludes the story by telling that when the other snail's family departs for another cabbage leaf, he is unable to move, and the poor snail soon fades and crumbles away. The young snail heeds his father's wise advice, vowing to keep his house small. As he explores the world around him, the dark earth, the mushrooms, the pine cones, and the trees, the young snail soon finds that he does indeed live in "the biggest house in the world."

Lionni, Leo. (1968). *Swimmy*. New York: Pantheon.

Swimmy is the only black fish among a school of red fish. He suddenly finds himself all alone when the red fish are eaten by a tuna fish. Exploring the world, he soon finds another school of red fish, and he encourages them to leave the dark shade of rocks and weeds where they hide. He shows them how to swim together in the form of a larger fish with him serving as the eye. As a result, they are able to swim through the cool water in the sun, chasing the big fish away. In this story, Lionni effectively illustrates the power of teamwork.

Lionni, Leo. (1985). *Frederick's Fables: A Leo Lionni Treasury of Favorite Stories*. New York: Pantheon.

Thirteen of Leo Lionni's fables contained in one volume in a picture book format: *Frederick, Fish Is Fish, Alexander and the Wind-Up Mouse, The Biggest House in the World, Geraldine, The Music Mouse, Tico and the Golden Wings, Cornelius, Swimmy, In the Rabbitgarden, Theodore and the Talking Mushroom, A Color of His Own, The Greentail Mouse,* and *The Alphabet Tree*.

Lionni, Leo. (1970). *Fish Is Fish*. New York: Pantheon.

A minnow and tadpole are friends who swim among the weeds in the pond. As time passes, the tadpole becomes a frog, and the minnow grows into a fish. The frog soon departs to explore the world, leaving the fish to swim in the pond without him. When he returns to visit the fish, he tells the fish of birds, cows, and people. Eager to explore the world, too, the fish jumps out onto the bank of the pond where he gasps for air, unable to breathe or move. The frog arrives to save his friend, pushes him back into the water, whereupon the fish learns to truly appreciate the beauty of his own world beneath the pond. The picture book format of Lionni's story is rich with underlying meaning embedded in the illustrations and the text from where the reader infers the moral of the story.

Lionni, Leo. (1985). *It's Mine*. New York: Pantheon.

Milton, Rupert, and Lydia, three quarrelsome frogs, live on an island. They constantly argue over the water, the earth, and the air. One day, a toad visits from the other side of the island, cautioning them that they cannot continue to argue and bicker as they do. When rain fills the air, their island grows smaller and smaller until they finally all cling to the back of one rock rising above the water. The three huddle together, trembling from cold and fright, while sharing the same fears and hopes. When the waters subside, they find the rock is actually the big toad. The three jump back into the water, swimming side by side around the island, leaping after the butterflies together and resting in the weeds side by side. Through their experiences, they discover they can share the peace and beauty of their island together as friends.

Lionni, Leo. (1987). *Nicolas, Where Have You Been?* New York: Knopf.

Young mouse Nicolas sets out across the great meadow in search of a field of ripe red berries not discovered by the birds. Along the way, he is grabbed by the claws of a huge bird and carried high into the sky. Nicolas struggles to free himself, and he falls down into the nest belonging to a family of birds. Nicolas is astounded when the birds invite him to stay, feed him red berries, and accept him as one of their family. One day, Nicolas awakens to find the birds gone, and only a pile of red berries left behind in the nest. He decides to return home, where he tells his friends of his adventures. His friends initially denounce birds when they learn of the big bird that grabbed him, but they soon learn that "One bad bird doesn't make a flock," when Nicolas's bird friends bring them ripe red berries.

Lionni, Leo. (1989). *Tillie and the Wall*. New York: Pantheon.

Tillie encourages her friends to see what is on the other side of the big wall where they live. They try to climb it, poke a hole through it, and walk around it, all with no success. It is only when Tillie follows a worm's example and digs a hole underneath that she discovers mice, like her, living on the other side of the wall. After much celebrating, Tillie and her new friends return through the tunnel to see what her side of the wall looks like. From that day forward, the mice travel freely from one side of the wall to the other, all thanks to Tilly, who showed them the way.

Lobel, Arnold. (1980). *Fables*. New York: Harper and Row.

This is a collection of 20 fables written and illustrated by Lobel. The format of the book includes a page of text with the moral stated at the end of the story and a full-page illustration to complement the text. Lobel has fun writing stories to illustrate lessons, such as "It is the high and mighty who have the longest distance to fall," "Satisfaction comes to those who please themselves," "A child's conduct will reflect the ways of his parents," and many others.

Lowell, Susan. (1994). *Tortoise and the Jackrabbit*. Flagstaff, AZ: Northland.

Lowell and illustrator Jim Harris tell the tale of the tortoise and the hare with a southwestern flair. Tortoise awakens one spring morning, proclaiming she feels good and fast. Jackrabbit laughs at her, and claims he is the fastest runner in the desert, upon which Tortoise challenges him to a race. The other animals of the desert—Roadrunner, Tarantula, Skunk, Gila Monster, Eagle, Coyote, and even Javalinas—gather around to cheer them on as they race. True to the story, the slow, steady pace of the tortoise soon passes the sleeping form of Jackrabbit, and she makes it to the finish line first. The moral "Slow and steady wins the race" is embedded within the storyline.

Paxton, Tom. (1991). *Androcles and the Lion and Other Aesop's Fables*. New York: Morrow Books.

Ten fables are retold by Paxton and illustrated by Robert Rayevsky. Paxton, a singer and songwriter, retells the fables in verse. Among the titles are "The Wolf in Sheep's Clothing," "The Ant and the Dove," "The King of the Barnyard," and "The Wolf and the Crane." The fables range from five lines telling the story of "The Bald Knight" to several pages as in "Androcles and the Lion." Each fable has at least two full-page color illustrations. The morals are implied within the storyline.

Wildsmith, Brian. (1966). *The Hare and the Tortoise*. New York: Oxford University Press.

Based on the fable by La Fontaine, Wildsmith remains true to the storyline. The slow and steady pace of the tortoise as he passes the sleeping hare enables the tortoise to be the victor of the race.

Wildsmith, Brian. (1987). *The Little Wood Duck*. New York: Oxford University Press.

A little wood duck is born different from his brothers and sisters. He has one foot larger than the other, which causes him to swim around in circles. His brothers and sisters and the other animals of the forest make fun of him. The little wood duck turns out to be a hero when he causes a fox, waiting for the ducks to come ashore, to become dizzy and giddy from watching the little wood duck swim around in circles. He saves his brothers and sisters, and they promise never to tease him again.

Wildsmith, Brian. (1969). *The Miller, the Boy, and the Donkey*. New York: Oxford University Press.

A miller decided to take his donkey to market and sell him. He and his son decided to carry the donkey, so that the donkey's feet would not get dirty. Along the way, people offer their advice as to who should be riding the donkey. By the journey's end, the miller is weary from thinking about all the advice he was offered. "From now on," he confides to the boy, "I shall make up my own mind and stick to it."

Wildsmith, Brian. (1971). *Owl and the Woodpecker*. New York: Oxford University Press.

Woodpecker lived in a tree in the forest where he worked all day and slept at night. Owl lived in the tree next to Woodpecker, and Owl slept during the day and worked at night. Owl soon becomes angry at Woodpecker's incessant pecking, and screeches at him to stop his incessant pecking. A family of beavers arrive and begin gnawing at Owl's tree. When a great storm shakes the forest, it is Woodpecker who saves Owl's life, and they struggle to safety as the tree falls to the ground. Woodpecker and Owl become good friends, and Woodpecker helps Owl find another home in a quiet part of the forest.

Young, Richard, & Young, J. (1993). *African-American Folktales for Young Readers*. Little Rock, AR: August House.

This collection of folktales includes favorite stories from popular African and African American storytellers. Animal fables found in the book include: "Python and Lizard," "Mr. Frog Rides Mr. Elephant," "Brother Lion and Brother Man," and "How Br'er Rabbit Outsmarted the Frogs." The stories are longer than usual for fables, and the moral is implied as opposed to being explicitly stated at the end of the story. Students in grade 4 and higher will be successful reading this book independently, and the stories could be used as read-aloud material for all ages.

4.1 Events in Action

Directions:
1) Identify the key event in your fable.
2) Summarize the key event in four actions or less.
3) Draw a picture to illustrate each action.

Fable	
Key Event	

Summary of Actions	Possible Dialogue	Draft of Illustration
①	①	①
②	②	②
③	③	③
④	④	④

4.2 Comic Strip Template

Directions: 1) The strip can be organized to read from top to bottom or left to right.
2) You could use one or more of the blocks to create your strip.
3) When finished, the blocks can be cut apart and pasted onto construction paper.
4) Use the top strip for the title of your fable.
5) Remember: Reflect the key event and actions that represent the fable.

Title:	
Illustration and Dialogue	

4.3 Graphic Organizer for Fables Containing One Setting

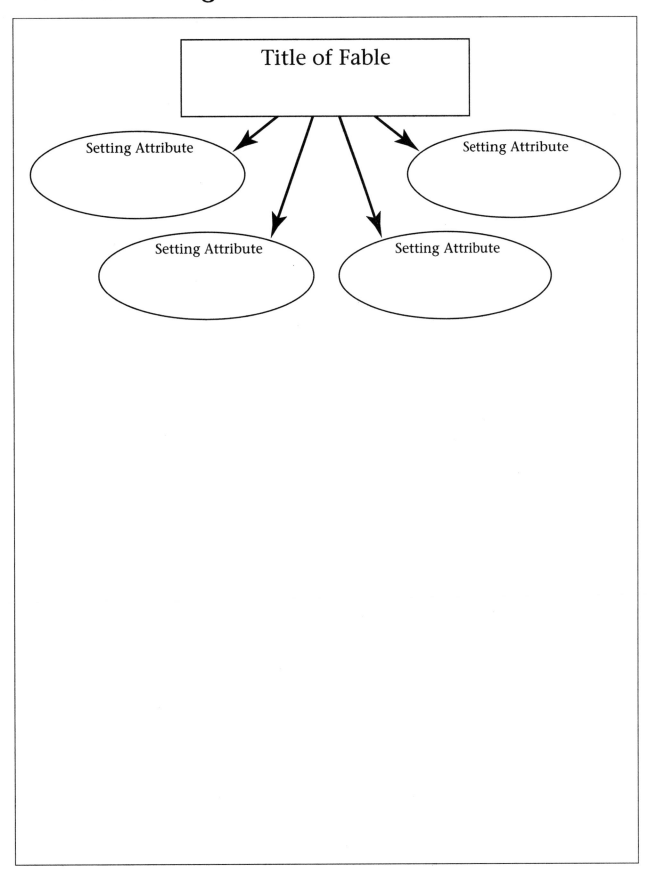

4.4   Graphic Organizer for Fables Containing Two Settings

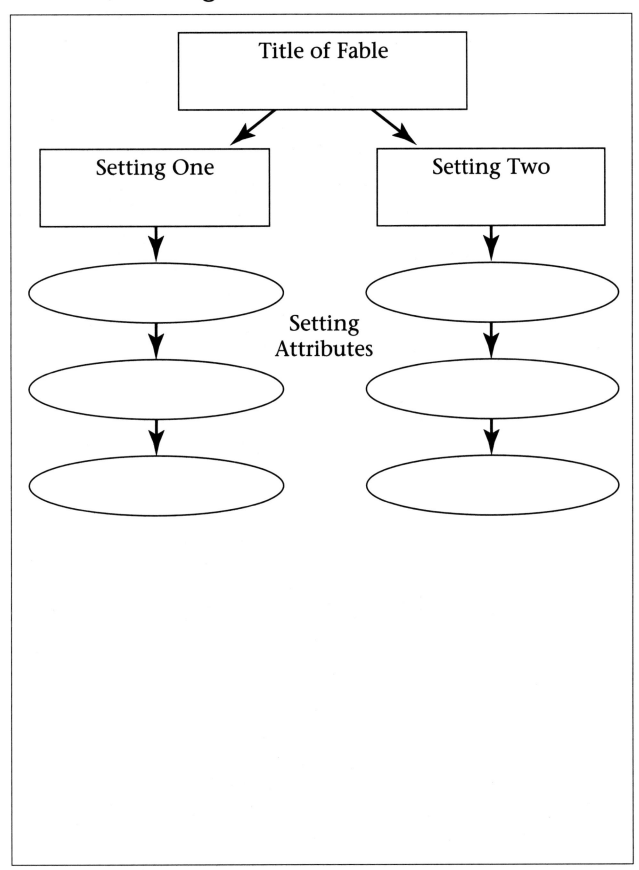

4.5　Fable Story Map

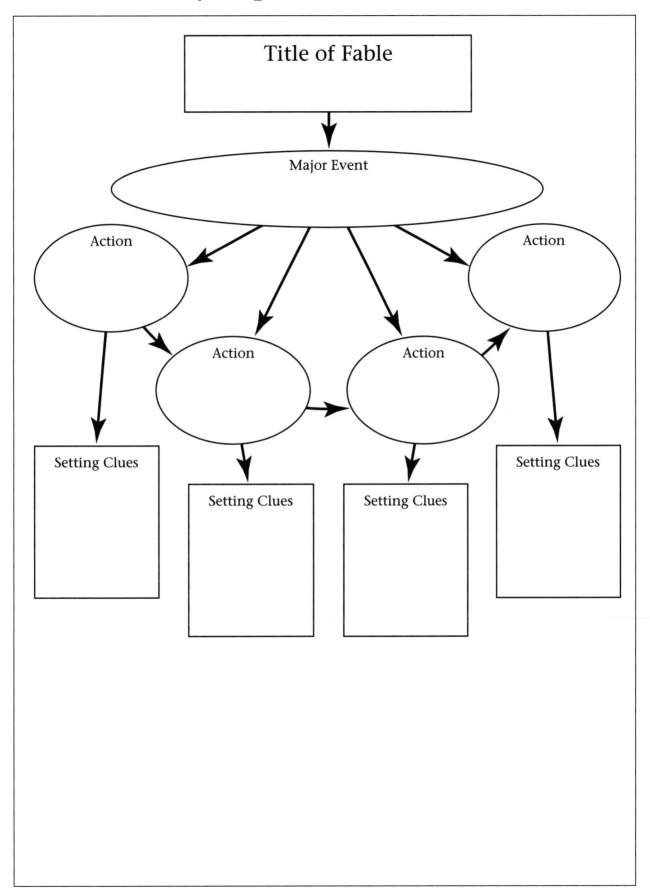

4.6 Character Trait Analysis

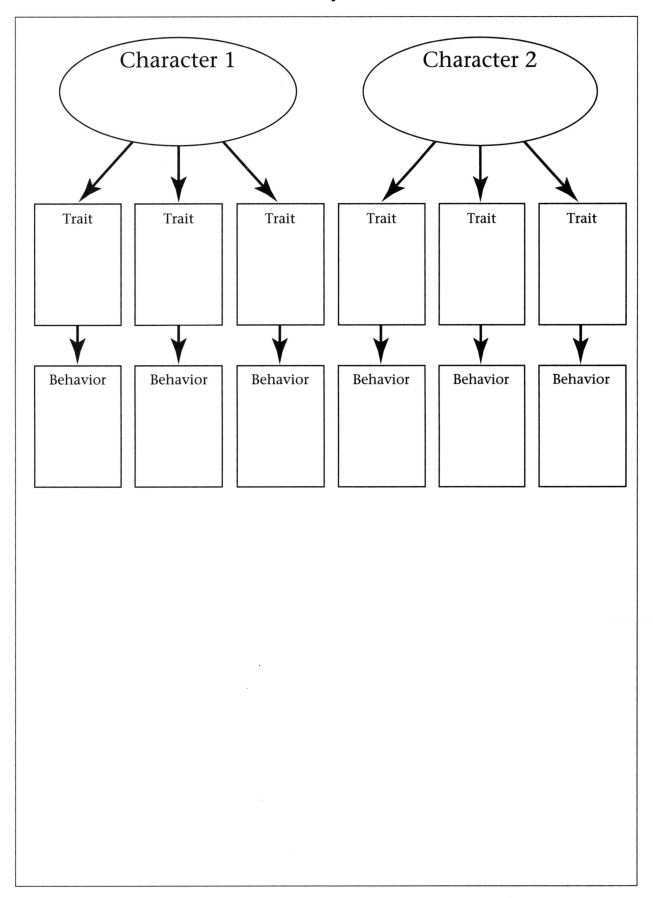

4.7 Puppet Theater Storyboard Notes

Directions: After reading your fable, use the organizer below to jot down notes to guide you in the construction of your puppet theater.

Characters		
Setting		
Major Event		

Key Actions	①	②	③	④

4.8 Storyboard Organizer for Comic Strip

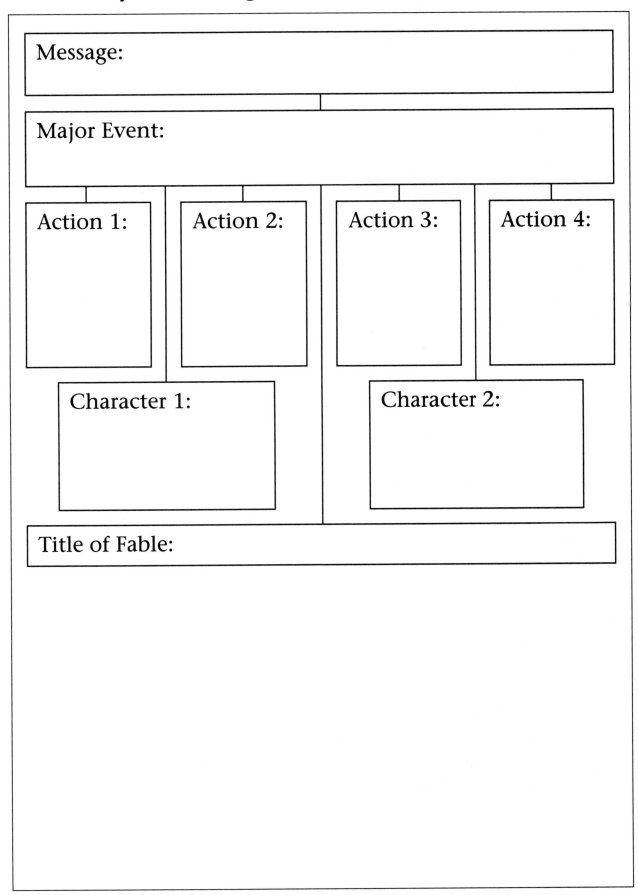

Message:

Major Event:

Action 1:

Action 2:

Action 3:

Action 4:

Character 1:

Character 2:

Title of Fable:

chapter **5**

All about Legends

What Is a Legend?

Legends are folktales told as fact and are presumably believed to be true by the storyteller (Bosma, 1987). These stories have been passed down from generation to generation and are thought to have some basis in history but are not verifiable (Tompkins & McGee, 1993). Although legends are not historical records, they do tend to include some mention of historical fact. This traditional narrative usually involves kings, heroes, or other important figures.

Distinguishing between Legend and Myth

In some ways, legends do resemble myths. Mythology evolved as primitive humans searched their imaginations and related events to forces as they sought explanation of the earth, sky, and human behavior (Huck, Hepler, & Hickman, 1987). In other words, it was how people sought to explain sacred beliefs. The principal characters are deities and supernatural powers, often with human attributes (Bosma, 1987). These characters deal with human relationships with the gods, the relationships of the gods among themselves, the way people accept or fulfill their destiny, and the struggle of people within and without themselves between good and evil forces (Huck, Hepler, & Hickman, 1987). The setting for myths is the remote past that deals with the creation of the world and the origin of natural events (Bosma, 1987).

In contrast to this, legends are based on real people and events, although the truth is sometimes distorted in the process (Bosma, 1987). In addition, the time setting for legends is in the present or the historical past in a recognizable world (Bosma, 1987). Like myths, legends also seek to explain sacred beliefs, and the focus shifts to humans, or animals acting like humans, telling the story as a way of glorifying their ancestry or history. The people in legends are concerned about the results of the conflict of natural phenomena. The nature of the legend can be sacred or secular, often concerned with changes in creation, transformation of humans and animals, or heroic deeds (Bosma, 1987).

In some references, legends are discussed within the category called *epic and legendary heroes* (Huck, Hepler, & Hickman, 1987) or *epic and hero tales* (Sutherland, 1997). For the purposes of this book, legend and myth will be discussed as two distinct and separate classifications of folklore (Bosma, 1987).

What Are the Characteristics of Legends?

The characteristics that legends have in common include:

■ The characters are often kings and queens, heroes and heroines, or other important figures in history; there is some historical connection to actual people.
■ The setting is usually in a historic time or place, in a recognizable world.
■ The heroes/heroines sometimes have encounters with nature.
■ A legend can be explanatory or historical.
■ Legends reflect the attitudes and values of the group that created them.

Summary

Legends are a traditional folk narrative typically involving kings, heroes, or other important historical figures. Every society has created some legend that is associated with its people, since it is a way of reflecting and sharing their values and beliefs. Although legends do tend to distort the truth, they are based on real people and events.

Reading Legends: What Are Examples of Each Characteristic from Actual Legends?

CHARACTERISTIC: THE CHARACTERS ARE OFTEN KINGS, HEROES, OR OTHER IMPORTANT FIGURES IN HISTORY

The character's place in history can usually be found by seeking out such resources as encyclopedias that summarize their accomplishments, or books that detail their lives in more depth.

David Wisniewski's *Golem* provides an opportunity to explore the creation and role of the golem figure from Jewish history some 400 years ago. In the story, the golem is made of clay to be protector of the Jews being persecuted in Prague. According to legend, a revered Jewish teacher and scholar, Rabbi Judah Loew ben Bezalel, took his guidance from a dream he had when he prayed for deliverance for his people. Rabbi Loew's historical significance is mentioned in a book note included by Wisniewski. He states that the rabbi wrote extensively about religious issues, winning tolerance and respect from Christian clergy. A different rabbi, Rabbi Elijah of Chelm, Poland, was originally connected with the creation of the Golem. The author also recognizes that it was not until the 1700s that Rabbi Loew became the subject of these stories.

Summary: Golem is created from clay by the chief rabbi of Prague to protect the Jewish people of Prague from repression due to Christian intolerance.

In *Saint George and the Dragon,* Margaret Hodges retells the story of Saint George (?–303?) of Merry England who was loved everywhere for his courage and virtue. Historical references are made to George, Christian martyr, who was born in Cappadocia in eastern Asia Minor (Microsoft Encarta 97 Encyclopedia). According to legend, a pagan town was victimized by a dragon (representing the devil), which the inhabitants first attempted to placate by offerings of sheep and then by sacrifice of various community members (Microsoft Encarta 97 Encyclopedia). In Hodges's version of the story, the king's daughter, Una, sets out on a journey to find a champion for her people. She encounters the Red Cross Knight and persuades him to return and slay the dragon.

> *Summary:* Through acts of courage and virtue, a young knight is soon heralded as England's friend and patron saint.

The Legend of King Arthur by Robin Lister is a collection of 14 stories about this legendary figure. It refers to Arthur, semi-legendary sixth-century King of the Britons, who fought against the invading Anglo-Saxons (Microsoft Encarta 97 Encyclopedia). He and his queen, Guinevere, maintained a magnificent court at Caerleon-upon-Usk (perhaps the legendary Camelot) (Microsoft Encarta 97 Encyclopedia). The stories in Lister's book chronicle the life of Arthur as well as stories of the knights from his Fellowship of the Round Table.

> *Summary:* The story of how young Arthur is followed from the time he pulls the sword from the stone to his departure to the magic isle of Avalon.

FOCUS ACTIVITY: CHARACTERS ARE IMPORTANT FIGURES IN HISTORY

▪ Characteristic: The characters are often kings, heroes, or other important historical figures.
▪ Activity: Character shield
▪ Summary: Pertinent information about the character will be identified: family, friends, wishes, goals, and feelings.
▪ Materials: *Merlin and the Dragons* by Jane Yolen; Reproducible 5.1 (Character Shield)—large for class and small individual character shields; construction paper, markers

How Do You Do It?

After reading aloud and discussing *Merlin and the Dragons* by Jane Yolen to the students, use the character Emrys (Merlin) to model how to make a character shield. Brainstorm with the students possible categories that could be used on the character shield (e.g., family, friends, wishes/goals, feelings, journeys, special talents, physical attributes, etc.; see Figure 5.1). When students volunteer categories, ask them to provide an example of something about the character that could be used on the shield. Share with the students that it is often dependent on the book as to the types of categories that would best represent the character.

Once a variety of possibilities have been discussed, divide the students into small groups. Ask each group to select one of the categories to write and illustrate for the rest of the class. Let the students work together for about 15 to 20 minutes to complete this part of the activity. Ask groups to return to the front of the class so that all pieces of the character shield may be placed back together. As each group presents, they can tape their piece of the shield onto the large class shield. When groups present their part of the shield, remind them to explain the connection of the character to its place on the shield.

After groups have finished presenting their pieces of the shield, students may do this activity independently. It could be drawn into their reading log, they could use Reproducible 5.1 to do the character shield, or they could create their own shield with construction paper and markers.

FIGURE 5.1 Character Shield

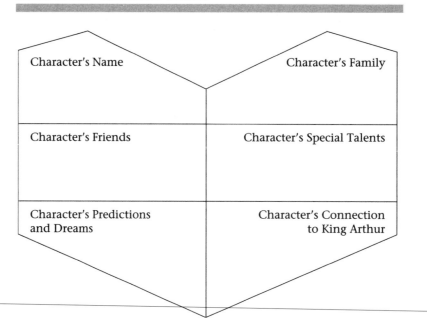

Extensions
1. Create a bulletin board of the character shields made by the students. Pairs of students can team up to select two characters (their own or other students' shields), and then compare and contrast the two characters on a Venn diagram or chart (see Figure 5.2).
2. In the folktale chapter (Chapter 3), a character trait analysis was done on a major character. This could also be done for the major characters represented in the legends.
3. Students could use their character shield to write a brief summary about the character.

   Note: This activity is a one-day activity when done as a whole class. If the students elect to make their own shields by working with partners or independently, they would need two to three days to draft and polish their shield.
   Reproducible master 5.1 may be found at the end of this chapter.

CHARACTERISTIC: THE SETTING IS USUALLY IN A HISTORIC TIME OR PLACE, IN A RECOGNIZABLE WORLD

From the sixth century and the days of King Arthur to the sixteenth century and tales of the Golem to the nineteenth century and Native American leg-

FIGURE 5.2 Venn Diagram

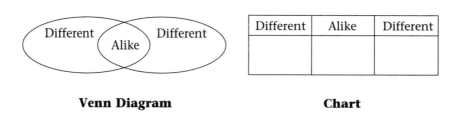

Venn Diagram   **Chart**

ends, each is an actual era of history. The people and their surroundings are depicted through text and illustrations to adequately represent the world.

Her Seven Brothers by Paul Goble is based on a Cheyenne legend involving the creation of the Big Dipper. This Native American legend is set in the Great Plains, and Goble's depiction of the birds, animals, and flowers are drawn to illustrate the region. In addition, his drawings of the tipis are taken from models that were made by Cheyennes in about 1900 for the Field Museum of Natural History in Chicago. The designs for the shirts and dresses are also based on actual Cheyenne design.

> *Summary:* The creation of the Big Dipper by the Cheyenne is told through Goble's "seamless interpretation of Plains Indian art and lore. "

The Legend of King Arthur by Robin Lister again provides a good example of a story that takes place in a historic time and place. The stories of King Arthur and the Knights of the Round Table are built around a legendary British leader from the sixth century. In the illustrations to the story, the castles, clothing, and mode of transportation are representative of that particular time in history. In addition, the strong religious associations and the search for the Holy Grail are truly part of that historic period.

> *Summary:* In sixth-century England, a legendary British leader and his followers embark on a quest for the Holy Grail.

Another book previously discussed, *Golem* by David Wisniewski, is based in the latter part of the sixteenth century. During this era in history, the Jewish people of Prague were confined to ghettos, walled areas in the city, and locked in at night. Entire Jewish populations were forced from their countries as a result of Christian intolerance during the thirteenth and fourteenth centuries, which served as a prelude to the events of the sixteenth century. Wisniewski includes in a final note at the end of the story that a historian, Jay Gonen, observed in his *Psychohistory of Zionism:* "Like the Golem, Israel was created to protect the physical safety of Jews through the use of physical power." Wisniewski concludes with the following statement: "In this allegorical fashion, Golem still lives."

> *Summary:* Rabbi Loew seeks to end the persecution of the Jewish people during the sixteenth century by creating the Golem, a man made of clay, to act as their champion.

FOCUS ACTIVITY: HISTORIC SETTING

▪	Characteristic:	The setting for the story is usually in a historic time or place, in a recognizable world.
▪	Activity:	Setting map
▪	Summary:	A setting map, depicting the background relevant to the particular time period, will be drawn.
▪	Materials:	*Golem* by David Wisniewski, construction paper, markers

How Do You Do It?

Read *Golem* by David Wisniewski as the initial introduction into a discussion of the setting of the story. Make a list of the points of focus throughout the book that give background into the setting of the story—for example:

- ▪ The river, Vltava, where they found the clay used to make Golem
- ▪ The walls of the ghetto
- ▪ Avenues of Prague
- ▪ The howling wind and rain lashing down as steam shrieked off Golem
- ▪ The walls of Rabbi Loew's attic study

■ The sunrise each morning
■ The storming of the walls of the ghetto and the shattered gates of Prague Castle
■ The cemetery
■ The synagogue attic

As this is done, it would help to move through the book again with the students, but this time focus on the background behind each illustration. Possible questions to ask include:

■ What is the overall background of the story?
■ Does it reflect a period in history in our world?
■ How is it recognizable to the world we know?
■ How does the setting of the story reflect what happens in each event?
■ How does the background change as the story progresses?

Decide what major areas could be represented on the setting map. For example, the walls of the ghetto behind which the Jewish people were forced to stay each night could be one area. Other potential areas to include could be the river, avenues of Prague, cemetery, synagogue, and Prague Castle. A trip to the library to seek resources to help in authentically representing the city of Prague would be helpful.

Next, decide how to represent each area on a draft of the map. Seeking other resources would be helpful here, too, since the placement of the river, the avenues of Prague, and Prague Castle can be more authentic as a result. It helps the students to gain a better understanding of the setting by validating the information. It also helps to reinforce the historic nature of the setting.

Divide the students into groups, and let them each take a different area of the map to create. Decide ahead of time how the map will be represented (e.g., three-dimensional, collage, or basic drawing). Ask them also to write on an index card a short summary that tells about the area. This writing task could be divided into two parts: (1) a short summary of what happens in the story in this particular area and (2) a short summary concerning historical information pertinent to the time and setting of the story.

When groups have finished developing the area and writing the summary, bring them back together as a whole class to put the setting map together. Adding other map features could be done at this time (e.g., map key or compass rose).

This activity next could be done as an independent or partner project related to books the students are reading in class. The students use the same guidelines followed when completing it as a class project.

Extensions
1. Students could do further research involving different types of intolerance chronicled through historical records (e.g., racial, religious, political, etc.).
2. Although the setting is historical, help the students work through fiction/fact represented in the book. For example, could the Golem have been made from clay?
3. Wisniewski's note included at the end of the story gives a lot of background information concerning the persecution of the Jewish people (e.g., where they must live, how they dressed, jobs they could or could not have, where they were buried, etc.). Have a class discussion of how it would feel to be treated this way.

Note: The activity as a group project may take one to two days to complete. It is dependent on how the areas are chosen to be represented. If a collage or three-dimensional techniques are used, it probably will take a bit longer than one day to develop. The students also need to write their summaries to accompany each area. If students elect to do the project as a partner or independent activity, then they will need up to a week, possibly longer, to do it well. This is especially true if the students are seeking other references to validate historic information on their setting map.

CHARACTERISTIC: THE HEROES/HEROINES SOMETIMES HAVE ENCOUNTERS WITH NATURE

This characteristic is especially evident in the legends of the Native American people. Through their stories, they tell of how earth's physical elements, as well as the stars and constellations in the sky, connect to the lives and history of the Indian people.

Ann Grifalconi's *Village of Round and Square Houses* is the story of a village that really exists. It lies in the remote hills of the Cameroons in Central Africa. Grifalconi shares how it is that the women live in round houses and the men live in square ones. The villagers were awakened one night by Naka, the mountain, groaning and rumbling. Through the night, Naka roared and grumbled, spewing lava, ashes, and smoke. The aftermath left everyone covered in a layer of soot, so that they all were unrecognizable. When Naka was finished, all that was left for the villagers were two houses, one round and one square. The Chief, unable to call his people by name, quickly assigned all the round, gray things to the round house, and the tall, gray things to the square house. And to this day, the custom remains.

Summary: The fury of Naka forces the village Chief to reassign his people to one of two houses left after the volcano is finished erupting.

Buffalo Woman, by Paul Goble, is based on a legend from the tribes of the Great Plains. The Buffalo Nation gives to a kind-hearted hunter a gift of a woman to be his wife. When the hunter's people refuse to accept her and their new son, she and the son flee back to the Buffalo Nation. Distraught that they have left, the young hunter follows them and proves his love by also joining the herd of buffalo as one of them. In order for the hunter to accomplish this transformation, he had to prove to the buffalo that he could recognize his wife and son amongst them. The buffalo then recognized his heart and courage by helping the hunter rid himself of his man-smell and making the buffalo robe he wore his new skin.

Summary: The relationship between man and animal and the power of love are illustrated through a hunter's courage in standing up to the Buffalo Nation in order to find his wife and son.

Tomie DePaola's book, *The Legend of the Bluebonnet,* is based on Comanche Indian lore of how the bluebonnet came to be. In this legend, it is the sacrifice of She-Who-Is-Alone that ends the drought and famine from which her people suffer. When the others in her tribe are instructed to give up their most prized possession, each makes an excuse not to give up a treasured bow or blanket. But the young orphan offers her warrior doll, the only reminder of her family, as a sacrifice to the Great Spirits. Her unselfishness is rewarded, and the hills become covered with bluebonnets everywhere the ashes of her warrior doll fell when she cast them into the wind.

Summary: A young girl's sacrifice of her most prized possession to the Great Spirits helps end the drought and famine from which her people suffer.

FOCUS ACTIVITY: ENCOUNTERS WITH NATURE

■ Characteristic: The heroes/heroines sometimes have encounters with nature.
■ Activity: Cause and effect relationships

▩ Summary: Using different cause and effect representations, the students will look at the conflict(s) characters had with nature.

▩ Materials: Ann Grifalconi's *Village of Round and Square Houses,* Reproducibles 5.2 through 5.5 (Cause/Effect Relationship) index cards, yarn

How Do You Do It?

Talk with the students about what is meant by cause and effect. Use examples to illustrate some simple and more complex examples (e.g., if you push the pedals on a bicycle, then the bicycle will begin to move). Ask students to provide their own examples. Share the variety of different graphic representations that may be used to illustrate cause and effect relationships (see Reproducibles 5.2 through 5.5). Encourage the students to brainstorm with partners examples from their everyday experiences to fit the different types of graphic representations. The students may come up with some other types of cause and effect relationships.

Ask the students to listen for some cause and effect relationships related to nature in Grifalconi's book, *The Village of Round and Square Houses.* Remind them that one of the characteristics of legends is that the characters sometimes have encounters with nature. After reading, discuss with students the role nature played in the development and outcome of the story (e.g., the volcano erupted and only two houses were left). Possible questions to use during this discussion are:

▩ When Gran'ma was telling the story, what did she mean when she said, "Old Naka began to groan and rumble and awoke from a long sleep!"?
▩ Why do you think the villagers were afraid?
▩ Why do you think "the black night was split open like a coconut"?
▩ What did the villagers do during this time?
▩ How did the villagers know when it was safe again?
▩ Why did the village chief say, "We must begin to rebuild our village now!"?
▩ What happened when they rebuilt the village?

Let the class work in small groups or partners. Ask them to select one of the graphic representations shown in Reproducibles 5.2 through 5.5 to illustrate a cause/effect relationship they identified in the story. Have each group share their illustrations. When students present their illustrations, be sure they answer why they decided to use a particular organizer. This is important, since it will help them talk through the cause/effect relationship. The different organizers can then be placed together in a sequential format to represent the order in which each happened in the story. Some possible interpretations may include:

▩ A chain reaction sequence was started by the eruption of the volcano.
▩ The eruption of the volcano (one cause) caused the people to be covered with ashes, the land to be covered with ashes, and the fields to be covered with gray stones (multiple effects).

It is possible also to combine different types of cause/effect relationships. Figure 5.3 combines a chain reaction with resulting multiple effects.

Note: It may be helpful for the graphic organizers to differentiate between cause and effect. Students could use color codes that use different colors to write, highlight, or circle the text. The students can easily draw their own graphic organizers using a different shape for cause (e.g., circle) and effect (e.g., square).

**FIGURE 5.3   Cause/Effect Relationship Shown by Chain Reaction
Sequence with Resulting Multiple Effects**

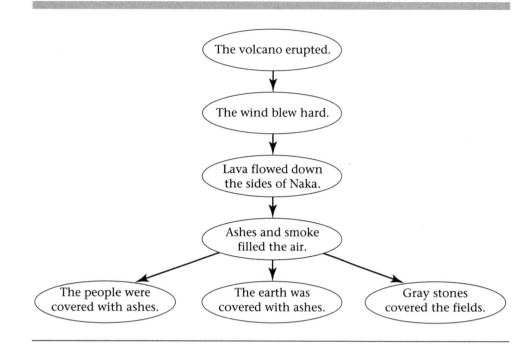

Extensions

1. Once students are comfortable and successful in identifying the cause/
   effect relationships from Grifalconi's book, they are ready to select a different legend (possibly one they are already reading in reading workshop),
   and identify a type of cause/effect relationship related to the character's
   encounter with nature. It can be recorded in their reading logs, and
   checked by the teacher during individual conference time.
2. A memory game can be made using simple cause/effect relationships to
   reinforce this skill. One card would have the cause written on it (e.g., Your
   feet push the pedals on a bicycle...), and another card would have the
   effect (e.g., ...and it begins to move). Students take turns turning over
   each card to try and find a match. The student with the most matched
   pairs wins the game.

Note: This lesson works well as a mini-lesson activity. It can be done in less
than 15 minutes when the students draw representations on the board or overhead as the class discusses the encounters between the character(s) and nature.
It will take longer to complete if the students meet together to discuss and illustrate some different cause/effect relationships they heard while listening to the
book. This is due to the fact they need time to discuss, reach a consensus, and
write and illustrate their graphic. It could easily be done in a regular class period
if done this way.

Reproducible masters 5.2 through 5.5 may be found at the end of this chapter.

CHARACTERISTIC: A LEGEND CAN BE
EXPLANATORY OR HISTORICAL

In most cases, there is some historical connection reflected within the legend.
Some of the Native American legends could be considered explanatory, since
they provide an interpretation of nature's role in their lives. In other cases, the
tales are historical in that they have connections to actual events in history
(although these events may sometimes be distorted). The origins of the Mam-

luk carpet in DePaola's tale and the legendary stories of Arthur and his Knights of the Round Table are representative of this connection.

The Star Maiden by Barbara Ruth Esbensen offers an explanation of how the Star Maiden and her sisters sought a home in the waters of the lake close to the Ojibway people. In so doing, they took the form of water lilies, representing glittering points of light on the lake. The petals of the water lily would shine in the sun, resembling the stars that lived and sparkled in the sky. Esbensen's version of this story is based on the 1850 work by the Ojibway Chief Kah-ge-ga-gah-bowh. This chief wanted to share in writing the history, customs, and legends of the Ojibway history, because he was afraid this information would disappear completely one day.

Summary: This Ojibway tale tells of the connection between water lilies and the stars that once shined high in the sky.

Merlin and the Dragons is a story by Jane Yolen that tells of young Merlin, and how his future becomes intertwined with Arthur, the future King of England. An older Merlin shares this story with young Arthur as his way of letting Arthur know he is the son of Uther and the rightful heir to the throne of England. From Merlin, Arthur hears of Emrys, a boy gifted in making prophecies, and how Emrys's dream of two dragons was intertwined with his future. It is through the battle between the dragons, and the subsequent battle between Vortigern and Uther Pendragon, that Uther becomes king and Emrys (later known as Merlin) becomes his wizard entrusted with the care of young Arthur.

Summary: This is an explanation of how Merlin's dreams prophesized his meeting with Uther Pendragon, father of Arthur.

King Arthur and Knights of the Round Table by Marcia Williams provides 13 stories involving figures connected with the legend of King Arthur. The relationships between Arthur, Guinevere, Lancelot, and Morgan Le Fay, as well as the quests they undertake and their search for the Holy Grail that consume Arthur and the Knights of the Round Table, are discussed throughout the book. The tales are explanatory narratives of different people and episodes associated with this legendary figure.

Summary: Thirteen stories chronicle the life of King Arthur through the connections he had with his family, Merlin, and the Knights of the Round Table.

The Legend of the Persian Carpet by Tomie DePaola explores the connection of a Mamluk carpet from the sixteenth century with a Persian legend. DePaola's story tells how the carpet, its pattern resembling a landscape of jewels, was a gift from the people of Persia to their king, Balash. After a thief steals a precious diamond that reflects on the walls the colors of the rainbow and accidentally shatters the diamond in the desert, the king vows never to step back into his darkened palace. A young weaver apprentice, Payam, convinced the king to return for a year and a day. The king reluctantly agrees, and the boy, with the help of the other young apprentices and the master weavers, agreed to "make a carpet as miraculous as the one our king stares at on the rocky plain." They are successful in their task, and the king's walls are once again filled with the colors of the rainbow from the reflections of the reds, golds, blues, and greens of the silk carpet.

Summary: The connection between a Mamluk carpet from the sixteenth century and an old Persian legend is offered through a story about King Balash of Persia, his shattered diamond, and the replacement lovingly offered by his people.

FOCUS ACTIVITY: EXPLANATORY OR HISTORICAL

■ Characteristic: A legend may be explanatory or historical.

■ Activity:	Time line
■ Summary:	A time line will be made to illustrate a sequence of events.
■ Materials:	Books about King Arthur, scratch paper, construction paper, markers, crayons

How Do You Do It?

Discuss the concept of time lines by using something familiar to the students (e.g., the school year, their own lives, daily events, etc.). Differentiate between a *flow* time line and a *graph* time line (Moline, 1995): In a flow time line, the steps in the sequence are joined by arrows. Little attention is given to the exact time period that has passed between each stage. In a graph time line, the periods of time are measured in equal units along a scale, allowing the reader to calculate more exactly how much time has passed between different points along the line.

Working in groups of two or three, students can select a story they would like to research in more depth. Possible stories include:

- ■ Merlin
- ■ Aurelius
- ■ Uther Pendragon
- ■ Arthur (as a boy)
- ■ Arthur (as king)
- ■ The Sword in the Stone
- ■ Guinevere
- ■ Lancelot
- ■ Knights of the Round Table
- ■ The Holy Grail
- ■ Mordred

The students can read from the different books about King Arthur to find information for their particular story. Before they begin the task, decide as a class on a possible format for the collection of information:

1. How will the information be recorded? (e.g., on index cards, paper, construction paper)?
2. How many key events from each story should each group find?
3. Will sources of each piece of information be noted on the cards (e.g., Merlin meets Uther Pendragon in Yolen's book *Merlin and the Dragons*)?
4. How will conflicting information within a group and between groups be resolved (e.g., in Yolen's book, Merlin (Emrys) meets Uther when Uther defeats Vortigern, but in Lister's book, it is Aurelius and Uther who defeat Vortigern)?

As groups finish, a rough time line can be started by using the floor or a wall. Students should approximate where they think their cards of information should go on the time line wall. After all the cards are displayed, the students need to examine the events shown to determine if everything is in the correct place according to when it occurred (e.g., Arthur did not meet Guinevere until after he became king, so anything to do with Guinevere should be after that particular point).

At this time, the class can decide whether a flow time line or a graph time line would work best for their display. Students can then work to space out their cards accordingly. Illustrations can be made to accompany various points on the time line. Once this has been accomplished, each group can present their portion of the time line to the whole class.

Extension

1. Organize a class scavenger hunt for different information that can be obtained by reading from the time line wall. Each group could be responsible for supplying two to three items on the scavenger hunt list. Every day several more items can be given out for groups to find and note on their record sheet.

Note: By introducing the concept of time line and how to do it on the first day, the students would be ready to move into their research by the next day. However, this part of the activity will take time for the students to research and organize their information. They will need two to three days to gather and record, followed by another one to two days for the groups to work together to organize the wall into a class time line. Add some additional time for the illustration. On the last day, the groups can present their portions of the time line to the rest of the class.

CHARACTERISTIC: LEGENDS REFLECT THE ATTITUDES AND VALUES OF THE GROUP THAT CREATED THEM

From the legends that impart the significance of the relationship between humans and animals to the conduct codes followed in the ancient days of chivalry, each story provides a glimpse into the type of people that created the story.

John Steptoe's *The Story of Jumping Mouse* is based on a moral tale originating among the Native American people of the Northern Plains. This story takes the smallest and humblest of creatures, a mouse, and shows how he can become the "noblest of creatures" by being true to himself and keeping hope alive within. Through acts of compassion, Jumping Mouse stops on his journey to the far-off land to offer his own sense of sight and smell to two creatures doomed to die. The bison cannot see to find grass and the wolf cannot smell to find food. Jumping Mouse is rewarded when the two creatures each help him further along on his journey. Jumping Mouse's unselfish spirit caused him to feel compassion for others less fortunate and helped to keep the hope alive within him as he traveled. The Magic Frog rewards Jumping Mouse by transforming him into an eagle free "to see the wondrous beauty of the world above and below and to smell the scent of the earth and sky and living things."

Summary: A small mouse's acts of compassion help him to maintain his unselfish spirit and remain true to himself as he journeys to the far-off land of his dreams.

Sir Gawain and the Loathly Lady, retold by Selina Hastings, represents the essence of chivalry from the days of King Arthur. Sir Gawain, seeking to save the honor of his king, offers to marry a lady of hideous countenance. Upon meeting the Loathly Lady, Sir Gawain gallantly asks for her hand in marriage. The wedding commences, and he gently leads his wife onto the dance floor to guide her through the steps of a dance. When they go upstairs to their chambers, the Loathly Lady is transformed into a beautiful woman. He is given a choice to have her beautiful by day or by night, and his response that she must choose whichever she prefers breaks the spell that bound her in the hideous shape of the Loathly Lady.

Summary: Sir Gawain's offer to save the honor of King Arthur finds him relying on the codes governing the ancient days of chivalry. His charity and selflessness are rewarded with the transformation of the Loathly Lady into a beautiful woman.

In *King Arthur and the Knights of the Round Table,* Marcia Williams includes several stories related to the knights' search for the Holy Grail. The Grail was the sacred cup used by Jesus Christ at the Last Supper. Legend has it that the Grail can bestow blessings on the good and punishment on the impure of heart or the irreverent (Microsoft Encarta 97 Encyclopedia). Williams shares the stories of King Arthur's knights, Sir Lancelot, Sir Percival, and Sir Galahad, and their quests for the Holy Grail.

Summary: The importance attached to the search for the Holy Grail is highlighted through stories of King Arthur's knights and their quests for the sacred cup.

FOCUS ACTIVITY: ATTITUDES AND VALUES

- Characteristic: Legends reflect the attitudes and values of the groups that created them.
- Activity: Attitudes and values (AV) map
- Summary: An AV map will be used to identify and reflect the attitudes and values important to the different cultures encountered while researching and learning about legends.
- Materials: Reproducible 5.6 (Attitudes and Values Map)

How Do You Do It?

Note: This activity can either be an ongoing activity throughout the reading of legends or it can be a culminating activity done toward the end of study. Students can gather information as they read if this is done as an ongoing activity. If done as a culminating activity, groups can take different cultures or be responsible for all of the cultures read about during the study of legends (e.g., People who are Jewish, British, Native American, African American, Hispanic American, European American, European, Asian, etc.). For the purposes of this lesson, it will be written as an ongoing activity.

Discuss with the students what is meant by attitudes and values. *Attitudes* relate to how a person behaves or acts toward something else. Here are examples:

- In *Buffalo Woman,* by Paul Goble, the hunter always gives thanks to the buffalo. His attitude toward the buffalo shows that he is a good and kind man.
- In *Sir Gawain and the Loathly Lady,* Sir Gawain treats the Loathly Lady with politeness and kindness.

Values refer to how highly regarded something is by a person. Here are examples:

- The hunter gives thanks to the buffalo for offering themselves to his tribe when they need meat. His practice of giving thanks to the buffalo relates to his attitude, but it is also reflective of how highly he values the buffalo.
- Sir Gawain's attitude toward the Loathly Lady shows that he values the courteous and charitable behaviors associated with the Knight's code of chivalry.

Let the students provide examples from their own lives that reflect their values and attitudes.

To study the different attitudes and values that are reflected in legends, refer to the attitudes and values (AV) map shown in Figure 5.4 (see also Reproducible 5.6). The AV map has been adapted from a character map shown in *Responses to Literature* by Macon, Bewell, and Vogt (1991). One side of the figure, representing Native American, is partially filled in to illustrate how to use the graphic organizer. In this case, the innermost square represents legends overall, the circles surrounding the square represent the differ-

FIGURE 5.4 AV (Attitudes and Values) Map

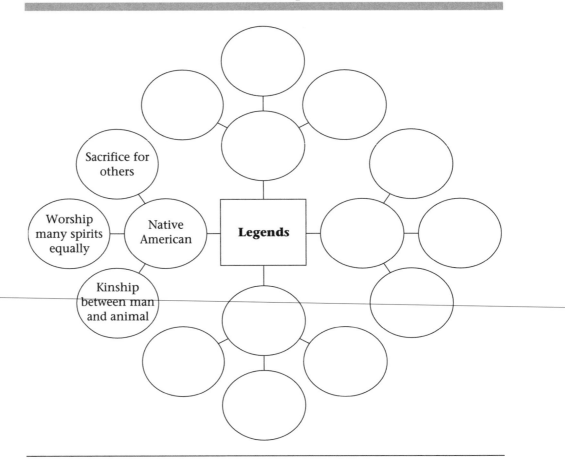

ent cultures encountered during the reading of legends, and the circles that extend out from each of these represent the different attitudes and values of each culture.

Since there are different Native American tribes represented in the many legends available, the class may decide to distinguish between them by identifying each tribe in the outermost ring of circles, and then extending more circles further out from these. Figure 5.5 illustrates one side of the AV diagram that draws from information available from Tomie DePaola's *Legend of the Bluebonnet*. The tribes that are associated with the same attitudes and values could be indicated by the students drawing a line from the circle back to the tribe.

Discuss once a week what could be added to the map. Possible questions to ask during this discussion include:

- ■ What books about legends did you read this week?
- ■ What cultures were reflected within the legend?
- ■ What clues were given by the author or illustrator as to the culture represented in the book?
- ■ Discuss the attitudes and values of each culture that were represented in the books.
- ■ What can be added to the AV map?
- ■ Where would this information go on the AV map? Why?
- ■ By writing this information on the AV map, what does it tell us about the culture?
- ■ What attitudes and values are shared across cultures? Make a list to reflect this.

FIGURE 5.5 Differentiating within a Culture on the AV Map

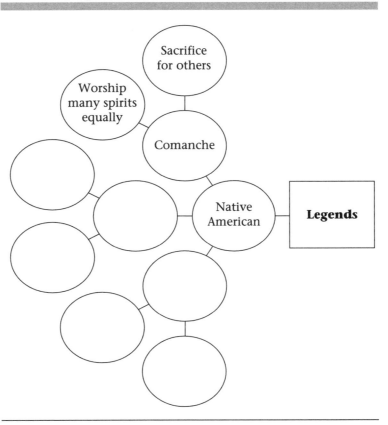

New information can be added by students writing on a transparency or the chalkboard, or the class can construct a wall AV map by using construction paper cut in half instead of circles.

At the end of the unit, examine what is listed for each culture. Are there any commonalities across the cultures? Do they share any attitudes and values?

Note: Encourage students to seek other sources of information to expand on what is embedded in the storyline of each legend. If they know *The Legend of the Bluebonnet* is about the Comanche tribe, they can go to the library or get on the Internet to find more information about this particular Native American tribe. Much of the information in each book must be inferred as the students read. In some cases, the authors have included notes at the beginning or end of the story that give more information about the origin of the book.

Extensions

1. Label each circle of the AV map as either *A* (attitude) or *V* (value). Discuss the connections that exist between the two (e.g., In *Buffalo Woman*, the hunter's attitude of giving thanks to the buffalo was his way of showing how highly regarded they were to his tribe).

2. Examine the AV map to determine what attitudes and values, if any, are shared across cultures.

3. Ask each student to create an AV map that reflects his or her attitudes and values.

4. Select a prominent person (e.g., the President of the United States) currently in the news, and identify what appears to be this person's attitudes and values based on what he or she does or says. Utilize newspapers, magazines, and Internet resources to document sources of information helpful in identifying these values and attitudes.

Note: This activity can either be ongoing during the study of legends or it can be done as a culminating activity. If it is done as an *ongoing* activity, consider the following: At the beginning of this unit, discuss the characteristics that are shared by legends. Next, move into a more in-depth discussion of attitudes and values using students' own life experiences to illustrate. Introduce the concept of the AV map as a way of presenting the attitudes and values of the cultures represented in each legend. One day a week, meet as a class to add new information to the AV map. Encourage the students to share any new information to be added, but also ask them to explain how it is they came to know it.

If the activity is a *culminating* one, consider the following: At the end of the unit, work together as a class to identify the attitudes and values of each culture represented in the legends.

Day One would consist of the discussion concerning what is meant by *attitudes* and *values*. Make a list of the different cultures the class read about during its study of legends. Groups of two to three students can select which culture they would like to represent on the AV map.

Days Two through Five allow the groups to begin looking back through the books that were read, or to seek out other resources to identify the attitudes and values of their culture. This gives students time to gather enough information to adequately represent their culture.

Day Six is when all the groups meet together to share and present their information to the rest of the class. Once all of the groups have finished and the AV map is complete, look for patterns across cultures.

Reproducible master 5.6 may be found at the end of this chapter.

Writing Your Own Legends

Using what they have learned about legends, the students can create a newspaper. Since the actual writing of a legend would be a challenge for many students, the students can instead take the information they have accumulated from different books they have read, organize it into various types of articles (e.g., news, editorial, entertainment), and then publish a class newspaper that shares aspects of what they have learned during their study of the genre. Working individually, with partners, or in groups, the students are responsible for providing the separate sections of the newspaper (e.g., news articles, editorials, advertisements) that focus on different aspects of legends. The class can decide to do this in one of several ways. The newspaper articles can be related to:

- One particular legend (e.g., Golem)
- Multiple stories connected with one legend (e.g., all the different stories associated with King Arthur and the Knights of the Round Table)
- A variety of legends (e.g., Golem, King Arthur, Legend of the Bluebonnet)

Students can write drafts of their articles by hand or compose on the computer using a word-processing program. Options for publishing the newspaper include:

- Organizing the articles by pages or sections on a wall of the classroom or school
- Selling photocopies to the school (be sure to obtain permission through the appropriate channels)

■ Handing out copies to other classes in the school
■ Sending home to parents as a way to inform them of what has been learned.

Activities for Writing

Figure 5.6 lists the activities used to illustrate the stages of writing and the recursive nature of the process that are included in this section.

FOCUS ACTIVITY: MAKING A NEWSPAPER
■ Activity: Making a class newspaper
■ Summary: The students will select the type of article they would like to write, and the articles will be combined into a class newspaper.
■ Materials: Newspapers, books concerning the different legends studied, construction paper, word-processing program and/or publishing program (optional)

How Do You Do It?

The first part of this activity is prewriting.

STAGE OF THE WRITING PROCESS
Prewriting   ■ Exploring the newspaper
■ Selecting the type of article
■ Making an outline

If the class has not previously studied newspapers during the course of the year, then it would be best to begin with some activities that allow students to explore elements of a newspaper. Select from the following list some activities that will help students become familiar with what types of information may be found in a newspaper:

■ Conduct a scavenger hunt by using the newspaper to find, cut out, and paste the following items in a newspaper log. Next to each item in the

FIGURE 5.6 Writing Stages with Corresponding Activities Related to Legends

WRITING STAGE	ACTIVITY
Prewriting	(1) Exploring the newspaper (2) What type of article will be written? (3) Outlining the article
Drafting	(4) Writing the article (5) Using the outline as a guide
Conferencing for content	(6) Using the outline as a checklist
→Revising	→Making changes
Conferencing for Conventions	(7) Color coding
→Revising	→Making changes
Publishing	(8) Class newspaper

log, write where it was found (e.g., section and page). For example, locate articles concerning:

— A letter to the editor
— A photograph with a caption
— Entertainment news article
— An editorial
— Local news
— A feature
— Sports news
— State news
— An editorial cartoon
— National news
— A commercial advertisement
— A listing from the classifies

■ Explore the layout of a newspaper by labeling the different parts. This can be done directly on a newspaper, or each part can be cut, pasted, and labeled onto a piece of construction paper. Parts of a newspaper related to the layout include the following (Brown, 1990):

— *Masthead:* Goes across the top of the front page; tells the name of the paper, where it is printed, and the date of the issue
— *Logo:* A slogan, design, or artwork that is the paper's trademark
— *Headline:* The large words above a story that introduce it
— *Banner:* The main headline on page one that tells about the main story of the day
— *Subhead:* A small headline that gives more information about a story
— *Byline:* Tells who wrote the story
— *Dateline:* Tells where the story happened
— *Caption:* The words under a picture that tell about it
— *Copy:* All the words in a paper
— *Index:* A table of contents for the paper, usually found on the front page.

Once students have explored the newspaper, they are ready to make some decisions about the type of news article they would like to write. Discuss how their study of legends could be used to do so. Since some students may need help in selecting the type of writing they would like to do, it would be helpful to brainstorm, as a class, different possibilities from which to choose. For example, they can take the basic type of news article and format it in a variety of ways. Some options include:

■ A feature article on King Arthur could be done by using an interview format. Either one student asks questions and supplies answers based on the readings about King Arthur, or a pair works together where one student poses as the king and the other interviews.

■ A news article could be done by conducting a survey. Students could survey other students in the school according to their favorite legend. The information can then be compiled and reported in a news article format.

■ Another news article format could be the latest news on the search for the Holy Grail.

■ A feature article could be done on popular foods, recipes, and cooking styles relative to the time period.

■ Other options include editorial cartoons, comics, and book reviews.

The use of newspapers as a means of connecting writing to legends can be emphasized in more depth by students taking on specific jobs (e.g., editor-in-chief, news department head, editorial department head, feature department head, sports department head, entertainment department head, art and photography department head, circulation manager, and person in charge of lay-out). For the purposes of this activity, the focus will be on writing different types of articles for the newspaper.

After students have decided on the type of article they would like to write, encourage them to outline their ideas to serve as a guide when they write. Reproducible 5.7 can be used as a basic guide for the students, although they may want to customize it to meet their own particular needs. For some types of articles selected, it may not be appropriate. Students can use articles that are similar by cutting them out from a newspaper to serve as a guide, too. Some overall tips to guide this process include (Brown, 1990):

- For news articles, remain objective and answer the 5 Ws (Who, What, Where, When, and Why) and How.
- Use a strong lead so that the reader is interested. For a news article, include as many of the 5 Ws and How in the lead as possible. For a feature article, catch a reader's attention quickly to draw him or her into a story.
- The most important information is included first, followed by the other paragraphs. The information that is least significant is presented last.
- The headline of the article should relay as much of the most important information as possible. This information is usually the same information (condensed) that is found in the lead paragraph.
- Students conducting interviews or surveys should prepare a list of questions beforehand.
- Direct quotes can be used to reflect a person's actual words. Be sure to punctuate correctly and identify the person who said it.

Each of these tips can be shared with the students in a 10- to 15-minute mini-lesson format. This gives the students the opportunity to familiarize themselves with the process before they have to try it themselves.

Mini-Lesson

Together with the class, write a news article concerning how King Arthur became King of England. Model how to complete the outline (Reproducible 5.7) to record basic thoughts and ideas.

STAGE OF THE WRITING PROCESS

Drafting
- Writing the article
- Using the outline as a guide

Using the outline as a guide, the students are now ready to write the article. Encourage them to utilize the legends as a resource when they write. If the students have spent the time to plan and outline their thoughts and ideas, then it simply becomes a matter of expanding the short phrases and sentences into cohesive paragraphs with transitions between each paragraph in the article.

Mini-Lesson

Use the outline from the previous mini-lesson to show the students how to take the basic ideas and expand them to write the news article. The use of an overhead or large chart paper and markers is helpful in modeling this process. This is also a good opportunity to show how to seek out other resources (e.g., dictionary, thesaurus, etc.). The focus at this point should be getting down the ideas; however, the students are expected to be accountable for conventions of writing (capitalization, usage, punctuation, and spelling) they have mastered already.

STAGE OF THE WRITING PROCESS

Conferencing for Content　　　■ Using the outline as a checklist

Students may need to conference as they are drafting or when they have completed writing the draft. If students have finished their drafting, it is important they check to determine if they included necessary elements in their article. They can use their outline to ensure that all elements have been included. Each item of the outline can literally be checked off, or the students can check or circle the information to indicate where it is found in the article. Students need to also check for cohesiveness, continuity, and transitions between the ideas and paragraphs they have included in the article.

Once they have completed a round of self-editing/checking, then they are ready for another pair of ears to listen and offer feedback. This can be accomplished in a group conference session, in a peer conference session, or by conferencing with the teacher. Regardless of the option chosen, the outline can again serve as a checkpoint for the students, or the students can use reference questions that are more general (Stewig & Jeff-Simpson, 1995), such as the following:

- What is this about?
- Where are you in the draft?
- What will you do next with the piece?
- What part do you like best?
- How did you happen to get into this subject?

The feedback may simply be oral, but students can also have the option of writing the feedback on the outline sheet. Items included on the conference sheet that were not on the original outline sheet are:

- It does not make sense when . . .
- You need more information about . . .
- I didn't understand . . .
- I thought _____ was really good.

Other questions that may be useful for the students to ask in their writing conferences include (Atwell, 1987):

- What's the most important thing you are trying to say?
- What's your favorite part? How can you build on it?
- What else do you know about your topic?
- Is all this information important to your reader? What parts don't you need?
- Does this lead bring your reader right into the piece?

Using these types of questions as a guide helps the students give each other valuable feedback that will be useful in making improvements in the drafts of their writing.

Mini-Lesson

Meet as a whole class or in small groups in order to model how to conduct a conferencing session. The questions on the conference sheet (Reproducible 5.8) or outline sheet (Reproducible 5.7) can be used as reference points.

Modeling how to conduct a writing conference can also be accomplished by sitting in on the conference session itself, but, at some point, the students need to be capable of doing it themselves. At any rate, model how to ask questions and give feedback in a manner that is not hurtful to the writer/author. It is also important for the students to realize they should also compliment the writer on what was done well. Students need to be responsible for taking the feedback from their "conferencing for conventions" session and improving their draft for the news article.

Mini-Lesson

Using feedback from a conference session, walk through, step by step, how improvements to the content of the drafts can be made. Cutting and pasting as well as using editing marks as shortcuts, instead of erasing and continuously rewriting fresh drafts, are useful (see Figure 3.13 for more information on editing marks):

- A line through an uppercase letter indicates it should be changed to lowercase.
- Three short lines underneath a letter indicates it needs to be capitalized.
- A circle indicates to omit something. (Words, sentences, or entire paragraphs can be deleted in this way.)
- A small arrow or caret symbol (^) indicates to insert.
- A cursive e-shape indicates to delete.
- Use the paragraph symbol to make a new paragraph (¶)

STAGE OF THE WRITING PROCESS

Conferencing for Conventions   ■ Color-coding

It is important for students to be responsible for conventions they have already mastered, but they also need to become aware of conventions in which they need improvement. If they do not know how to do a certain conventional skill, such as use quotation marks in dialogue, then they are not going to know how to correct it when they self-edit. This is when teacher mini-lessons on different skills and strategies becomes extremely important.

Mini-Lesson

These mini-lessons can be emphasized as relating to conventions of writing the students may encounter during the writing of their newspaper article:

- Using quotation marks and dialogue
- Using commas
- Listening to their text so they can assess which conventions they need and where (Graves, 1994)
- Interchanging pronouns and nouns
- Using strong verbs
- Proofreading using editing marks
- Using capitals for proper nouns
- Using apostrophes with possessives
- Combining sentences

Select one or two conventions at a time upon which to focus. Use a piece of your own writing, another student's paper (ask for permission first), or an excerpt from a book to highlight each of the conventions. For example, use a page from the book *The Legends of King Arthur* by Robin Lister. In the "Tintagel" story from Lister's book, focus on the use of quotation marks, commas, and ways to say *said* (e.g., *stammered, replied, barked,* etc.).

Using a variation of an approach taught by Joyce Armstrong Carroll (Carroll, 1982), ratiocination, the students can color-code their drafts for different conventions of their writing that need to be corrected. Color-coding simply means to assign a certain color (e.g., red) and symbol (e.g., circle) to a convention of writing (e.g., spelling) that needs to be corrected. For instance, if a word is misspelled, then it can be circled in red to indicate it needs to be changed. It is best not to select so many color codes that the students gets confused. A color-code key (Figure 5.7) is helpful in keeping track of what the students intend to focus on when looking through the drafts.

The students can write their keys in a corner of their papers to help them keep track of their codes. To color-code a draft, the students move through one code at a time. This ensures that their focus remains on that one particular convention of writing. The only exception to this is if they use the green/red color code to indicate capital letter/ending punctuation for each of their sentences. If they complete the green/red sequence, it is easier to see that one or the other is missing. Emphasize that the green color represents go and the red color represents stop. If there are repetitive green colors with no red color in between, then that means there is ending punctuation missing from their sentences. For the other codes (e.g., spelling, repetitiveness), it is best to move completely through the paper, focusing on one code at a time before moving onto another code. This technique can be used to self-edit and peer-edit. Once students have completed the self-editing and/or peer-editing for conventions of writing, they are ready to rewrite and polish their drafts. A final meeting with the teacher as a quality checkpoint will ensure that the pieces have been polished and are ready for publication.

STAGE OF THE WRITING PROCESS

Publishing   ■ Planning the layout of the newspaper
              ■ Pulling the newspaper together

Once all drafts are rewritten, the class can begin planning the layout of the newspaper. If many articles are available for the newspaper, yet resources are limited for including all articles in the paper, then the class could have separate specialty sections (e.g, features, news, entertainment) or the articles could be divided into several newspapers.

On the final printing of the newspaper, encourage each writer to present his or her article to the class or other classes. An important part of the publishing process is to share with a real audience.

FIGURE 5.7   Sample Key for Color-Coding When Editing for Capitalization, Punctuation, Spelling, and Repetitiveness

Color	Code	Convention
Green	Trace over letter	Capital letter at beginning of sentence
Red	Trace over ending punctuation	Punctuation at end of sentence
Yellow	Highlight	Spelling
Blue	Repetitive words	Very, too

Note: This lesson can be two to three weeks or longer. It is dependent on how much of the students' work is done in class or out of class. If done in class, then the following time line may be helpful:

Days One and Two involve the exploration of the newspaper.

Days Three and Four allow the students to select the type of article they would like to write, find guideline articles in the newspaper (for formatting), and make an outline of their thoughts and ideas.

Days Five and Six are devoted to the students to begin writing their articles.

Days Seven and Eight involve conferencing for content to get feedback on the articles and making improvements accordingly.

Days Nine and Ten allow the students to meet in conferences to concentrate on conventions of writing. They need also to make corrections based on this feedback.

Days Eleven and Twelve involve polishing the story, rewriting it, and ensuring it is ready for publication. The teacher as a final quality checkpoint is important.

Day Thirteen is spent with the students coordinating the articles into the newspaper, and presenting the newspaper to the class and other classes.

Reproducible masters 5.7 and 5.8 may be found at the end of this chapter.

Tieing in to Technology

INTERNET CONNECTIONS

Internet sites that contain links to information concerning Arthurian legend include the following:

■ http://reality.sgi.com/employees/chris_manchester/arthur.html
This site answers frequently asked questions about Arthurian legend, and it includes a list of knights and an explanation of the shields. It also has additional links to other Arthur sites around the globe.

■ http://rodent.lib.rochester.edu/camelot/cphome.stm
Called the Camelot Project, this site includes Arthurian texts, images, bibliographies, as well as basic information.

■ http://www.cua.edu/www/hist/netserf/home.htm
NetSERF contains numerous links to medieval resources. Items of interest at this site relate to medieval archaeology, architecture, culture, drama, history, law, people, and more. This site is more suited to older students who could tie in an in-depth study of culture while studying this genre.

■ http://www.scils.rutgers.edu/special/kay/golem.html
Kay Vandergrift includes a link to David Wisniewski's *The Golem* at this site. She discusses initial questions that can be used to introduce the book as well as questions that may be raised by the text. Links are provided to background information on the Golem legend, alternative versions of the Golem written for children, websites on the Golem and related issues, and children's responses to the Golem.

■ http://www.scils.rutgers.edu/special/kay/native.html
Vandergrift also includes this link to a bibliography of Native American stories:

▪ http://www.acs.ucalgary.ca/~dkbrown/storfolk.html
Additional information on folklore, myth, and legend can be found at this Internet resource. This site contains links to myths and legends of the Sioux as well as a link to other old Indian legends.

CREATING A MAP

After students have finished reading one of the stories, they can create a map of the setting by using a draw or paint program on the computer. They can then label key places and create a key to read the map. Two good activities are:

▪ Create a map for the village in *The Village of Round and Square Houses* by Ann Grifalconi.
▪ Designate the route that will be traveled by individuals embarking on a quest for the Holy Grail.

PUBLISHING FORMATS

Many software programs allow young writers to move easily between creating images, writing text, and designing layout (Downes & Fatouros, 1995). Within these programs, there are numerous formats available from which students can choose—for example:

▪ Create a travel guide using a brochure format. The students can highlight key locations that will be visited by individuals undergoing a quest for the Holy Grail.
▪ Create a flier that depicts the major character(s) and theme for *The Legend of the Bluebonnet* and *The Legend of the Indian Paintbrush*, by Tomie DePaola, or *Her Seven Brothers*, by Paul Goble.
▪ Detail a calendar that recreates the events surrounding the explosion of the volcano in *The Village of Round and Square Houses*. The students return to the text for information, but they can also seek other resources to fill in the blanks concerning information before, during, and after the volcano's eruption. This project can be tied to the drawing of a map.
▪ Write a resume for King Arthur or Lancelot that highlights key information concerning their experiences.

Annotated Bibliography: Legends

Baker, Olaf. (1981). *Where the Buffalo Begin*. New York: Frederick Warne.
This Native American legend describes how a young Native American boy led the buffalo from the great lake to the south to save his people from attack by another tribe.

DePaola, Tomie. (1980). *The Legend of Old Befana*. New York: Harcourt Brace Jovanovich.
This is an Italian Christmas story of the celebration of Befana, who flies across the sky on the Twelfth Night, leaving cakes and cookies for children as they sleep.

DePaola, Tomie. (1983). *The Legend of the Bluebonnet*. New York: G. P. Putnam's Sons.
DePaola retells the old legend of the state flower of Texas based on Comanche Indian lore of She-Who-Is-Alone, a little girl who made a sacrifice to save her tribe. In order to end the drought and famine that is killing her people, She-Who-Is-Alone offers to the Great Spirits the only possession she has left from her family who died in the famine. As a result of her sacrifice, the hills become covered with Bluebonnets, a warm rain embraces the land, and her people change her name to One-Who-Dearly-Loved-Her-People.

DePaola, Tomie. (1988). *The Legend of the Indian Paintbrush.* New York: G. P. Putnam's Sons.

> DePaola shares how this plant, which covers the hills of Texas and Wyoming each spring, received its name by retelling an old Indian legend. A young Indian artist, Little Gopher, works throughout his life to fulfill the Dream-Vision that came to him as a young child. He paints pictures of great hunts and of great Dream-Visions, telling the stories of his people. His greatest gift is when he paints the colors of the sunsets which, in turn, cause the hills to be covered with the brilliant reds, oranges, and yellows of Indian Paintbrush. His people change his name from Little Gopher to He-Who-Brought-the-Sunset-to-the-Earth.

DePaola, Tomie. (1993). *The Legend of the Persian Carpet.* New York: G. P. Putnam's Sons.

> This story, retold by DePaola, is based on a "Persian legend that had long been associated with a sixteenth-century Mamluk Carpet, explaining its pattern, which looked like a landscape strewn with jewels." In this tale, a precious diamond is stolen by a thief from the generous King Balash. Payam, a weaver apprentice, finds the diamond broken into a thousand pieces in the desert. The distraught king vows never to step back into the dark palace again, instead promising to stay near the colors of the rainbow cast by the diamond fragments. Young Payam entices the king to return by promising to fill the "hall of the diamond" with beautiful colors. With the help of the other apprentices and weaver, they weave a silk carpet that fills the room with reflections of the colors of the rainbow.

Esbensen, Barbara Juster. (1988). *The Star Maiden: An Ojibway Tale.*

> This poetic retelling of the Ojibway legend of Star Maiden describes how she came from the skies as a star to make her home on Earth. The Ojibway people welcome her, but she is unable to find a peaceful resting place. She and her star-sisters finally settle in the calm waters over the lake and take the form of water lilies. The picture book format of the book includes text on left pages with illustrations by Helen K. Davie on the opposite right pages.

Esbensen, Barbara Juster. (1989). *Ladder to the Sky: How the Gift of Healing Came to the Ojibway Nation.* Boston: Little, Brown.

> A long time ago, the Ojibway people were strong and healthy, no one was ever sick, and no one died. A grandmother tries to follow her grandson to the spirit world by climbing the forbidden vine linking the earth with Manitou's great blue sky home. She tumbles to the ground and is faced with the wrath of her people. In turn, all of the Ojibway people must face the wrath of the Great Spirit. Their punishment is sickness and death, and they must learn how to heal themselves with the flowers and herbs of the earth.

Goble, Paul. (1984). *Buffalo Woman.* New York: Bradbury Press.

> Goble bases his story on a legend that comes from the tribes of the Great Plains. A buffalo cow is transformed into a beautiful woman as a gift from the Buffalo Nation to a kind-hearted young hunter. The woman becomes the wife of the hunter, and they have a son. Others in their village refuse to accept the mother and child, so they return to the herd in animal form. The hunter follows them into Buffalo Nation and proves his love by joining them as a buffalo. Through his story, Goble tells of a kinship between animal and man, and of the transfiguring power of love.

Goble, Paul. (1988). *Her Seven Brothers.* New York: Bradbury Press.

> This story shares the Cheyenne legend of the creation of the Big Dipper. A young girl, gifted in making shirts and moccasins beautifully decorated with porcupine quills, travels to the north country to find her seven brothers. She bestows upon them a gift of shirts and moccasins and stays to take care of them. When the Chief of the Buffalo Nation is enraged that the girl does not come see him as requested, his herd stampedes and the girl and her brothers must flee for their lives. With the power of the youngest brother, they climb a tree into the boundless star-prairies high above the earth where they form the seven stars of the Big Dipper. If one looks closely enough, the eighth star, that of the little brother, walks with his sister.

Grifalconi, Ann. (1986). *The Village of Round and Square Houses.* Boston: Little, Brown.

> This is an African legend of a real village in the remote hills of the Cameroons in Central Africa. It tells why the women live in round houses and the men live in square houses in the village of Tos. Long ago, when Old Naka, the mountain, exploded, all that was spared were two houses. Since the people were all covered in ashes, everyone looked the same. So the village chief ordered all the round, gray things to live in the round houses, and all of the tall, gray things to live in the

square houses. The women decided they enjoyed getting together to laugh and talk and sing, and the men had become used to being together and relaxing in their own place. They continued the arrangement, since each had a place to be together and a place to be apart.

Hastings, Selina. (1987). *Sir Gawain and the Loathly Lady*. New York: William Morrow.
> The Black Knight will spare King Arthur's life if he can answer this question: What is it that most women desire? With the help of the Loathly Lady, Arthur is able to answer, but the price he must pay for the lady's help is to give her one of his brave knights to be her husband. Sir Gawain valiantly volunteers, and the fate of the Loathly Lady ties back to the same question Arthur had to answer for the Black Knight.

Hodges, Margaret. (1984). *Saint George and the Dragon*. Boston: Little, Brown.
> Hodges retells the legend of Saint George and the Dragon from Edmund Spenser's *Faerie Queene*. The story vividly illustrates the fierce battle between the Red Cross Knight and a dragon terrorizing the land. After numerous encounters, the knight successfully slays the dragon. To show his gratitude, the king offers him Una as his bride and promises that the Red Cross Knight also will become the next king. Through his acts of courage and virtue, such as that depicted in this story, the Red Cross Knight became known as Saint George of Merry England, England's friend and patron saint.

Lagerlöf, Selma. (1990). *The Legend of the Christmas Rose*. New York: Holiday House.
> This retelling by Ellin Greene of Lagerlöf's story was originally published in the December 1907 issue of *Good Housekeeping*. The Robber Family, banished to the forest by the bishop because of Robber Father's stealing a cow, witness each year the miracle of the forest turning into a beautiful garden to celebrate the remembrance of the Christ Child. In exchange for a visit to the forest garden, the abbot agrees to talk to the bishop to pardon Robber Father. The abbot goes to visit the Robber family, promising to return with a beautiful flower from the Christmas garden for the bishop. The outcome of this visit illustrates how faith can make miracles happen.

Lister, Robin. (1988). *The Legend of King Arthur*. New York: Doubleday Books.
> This collection of 14 stories chronicles the life of King Arthur. The stories begin with Merlin, then move into the arrival of Arthur, followed by the formation of the Fellowship of the Round Table. Other stories continue to retell the history of the legend of King Arthur. In general, the story length ranges from 4 to 12 pages, with some color illustrations interspersed throughout the text of the stories.

Shannon, Mark, & Shannon, David. (1994). *Gawain and the Green Knight*. New York: G. P. Putnam's Sons.
> Gawain, the youngest of King Arthur's knights, accepts a challenge from the mysterious Green Giant. When the Green Giant is victor of the first part of their match, Gawain is instructed to meet him in the enchanted north in one year's time. Gawain follows instructions and embarks on his journey, carrying a sash made by his beloved Caryn. Gawain successfully meets the challenge of the Green Knight, since his knightly passion, honesty, and courage ensured that he remained true to the mysteries of his own heart.

Steptoe, John. (1984). *The Story of Jumping Mouse*. New York: Lothrop, Lee, and Shepard.
> Steptoe gives his interpretation of a Native American legend of a young mouse who begins his journey to visit the far-off land. Along the way, he encounters a Magic Frog who bestows upon him the name Jumping Mouse. Magic Frog also tells him he will reach his destination by keeping hope alive within him. Jumping Mouse continues on his journey, and, through acts of compassion, gives his sense of sight and smell to other creatures in need. The unselfish spirit of Jumping Mouse is rewarded when he is changed into an eagle, free to "see the wondrous beauty of the world above and below and to smell the scent of earth and sky and living things."

Williams, Marcia. (1996). *King Arthur and the Knights of the Round Table*. Cambridge, MA: Candlewick Press.
> Marcia Williams retells the adventures of Camelot in a comic book format. Included are the stories of King Arthur, Excalibur, Morgan Le Fay, Guinevere and the Round Table, Sir Lancelot of the Lake, Sir Lancelot's First Quest, Princess Elaine, Sir Galahad, Sir Lancelot's Grail Quest, Sir Percival's Grail Quest, Sir Galahad's Grail Quest, and Camelot. Each story is presented in a two page format with boxed text and accompanying illustrations.

Wishniewski, David. (1996). *Golem*. New York: Clarion Books.

> Four hundred years ago, a giant man of clay was shaped and brought to life by a revered Jewish teacher and scholar, Rabbi Loew. The task of the golem was to protect the Jews, and take those who wish to harm them to the authorities. When a mob arrives to attack the outnumbered and weaponless Jewish people, the outcome of the golem's defense of them is too much death and destruction. In exchange for the safety of his people, Rabbi Loew promises to destroy the golem by returning him to the earth.

Yolen, Jane. (1995). *Merlin and the Dragons*. New York: Cobblehill Books.

> Merlin, guardian of young Arthur, shares with the king the story of his birthright. King Arthur learns of Urther's fight to become king, and how Uther sent Arthur away with Merlin for safekeeping. It was only after hearing the story of Emrys and Uther that Arthur no longer felt himself a fraud for having pulled the sword from the stone, thus fulfilling the legend, "Who pulleth out this sword from this stone is rightful king of England." The story is in picture book format, and the illustrations are beautifully done by Li Ming.

5.1 Character Shield

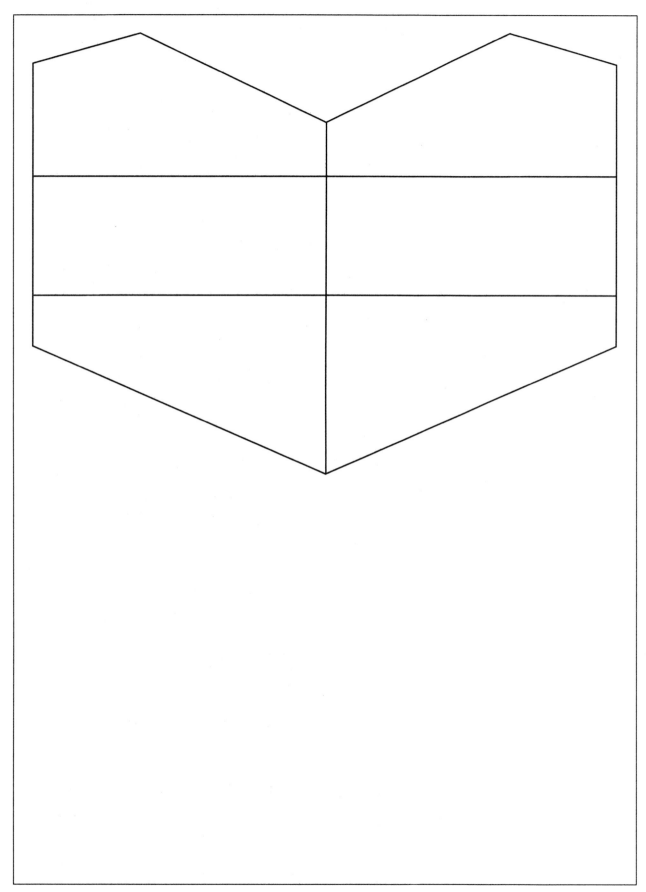

5.2 Cause/Effect Relationship

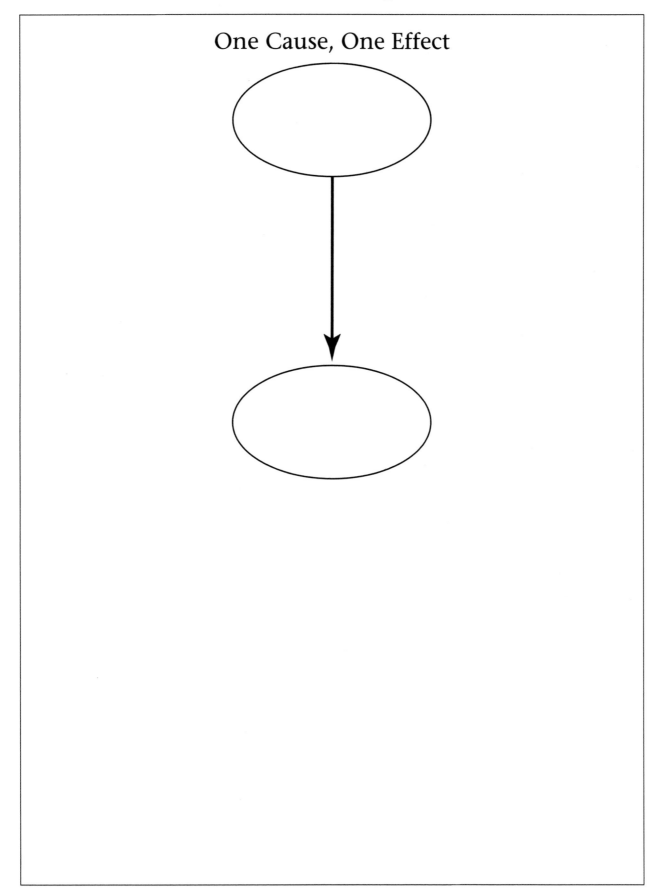

One Cause, One Effect

5.3   Cause/Effect Relationship

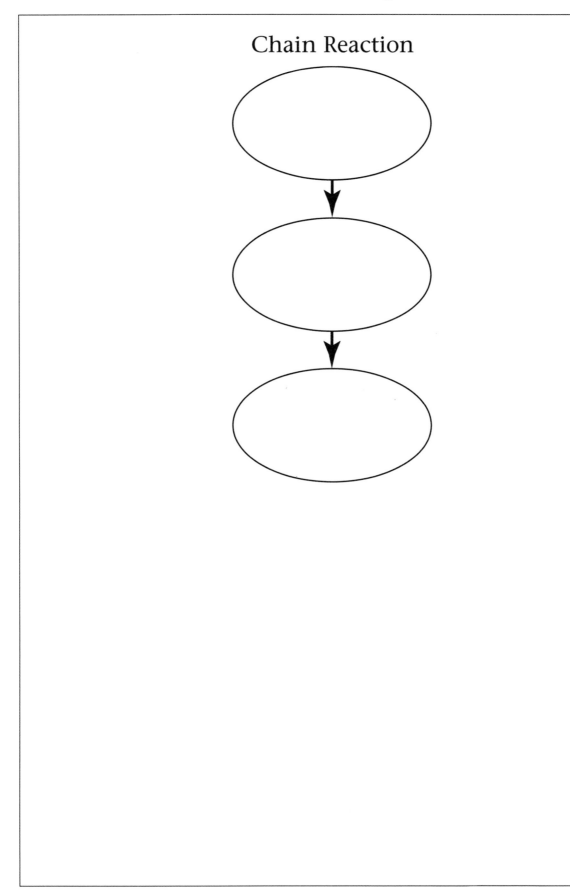

Chain Reaction

5.4 Cause/Effect Relationship

One Cause, Multiple Effects

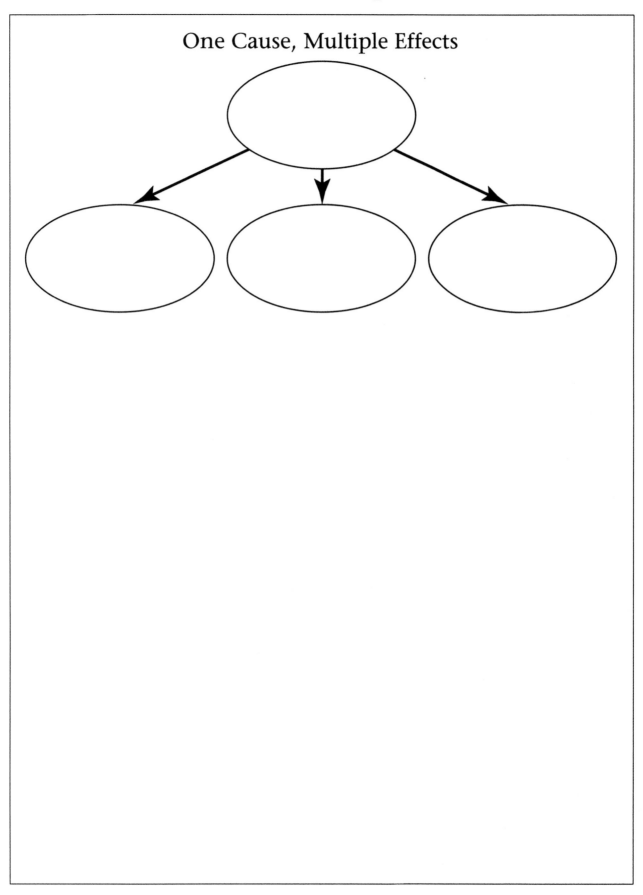

5.5   Cause/Effect Relationship

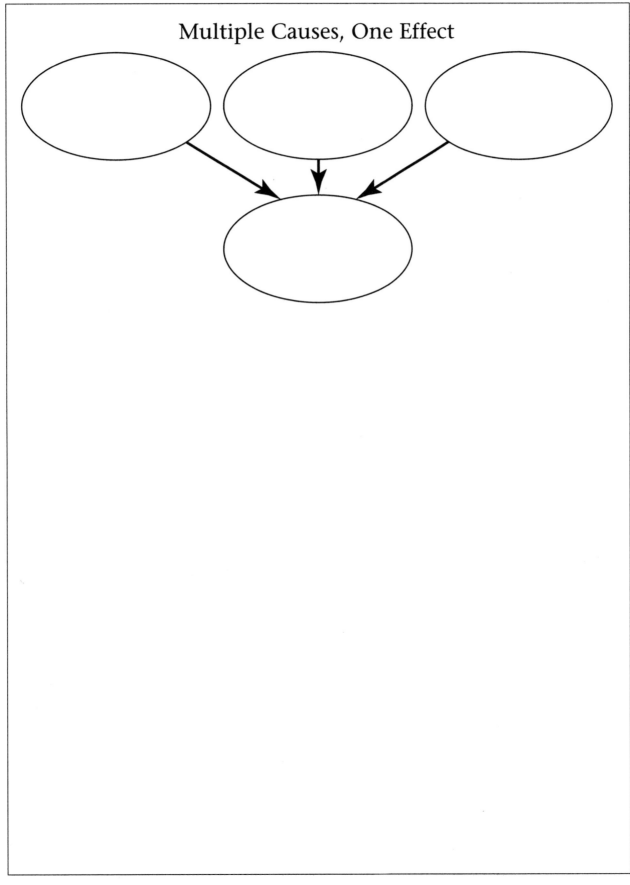

Multiple Causes, One Effect

5.6 Attitudes and Values (AV) Map

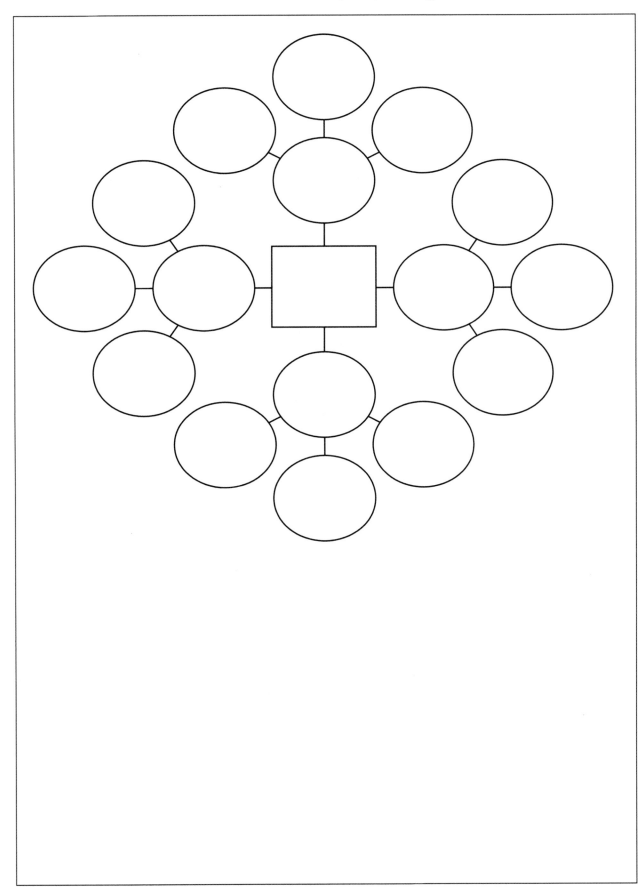

5.7 Outline for Newspaper Article

I. Type of Article _____

Newspaper Section_____

   A. Who
      1.
      2.
   B. What
      1.
      2.
   C. Where
      1.
      2.
   D. When
      1.
      2.
   E. Why
      1.
      2.
   F. How
      1.
      2.

II. Lead Sentence and Paragraph

   A. First sentence of article _____

_____

   B. Other important information for lead paragraph (specific information, direct quotes, etc.)
      1.
      2.
      3.
      4.
      5.
   C. Second paragraph (specific information, direct quotes, etc.)
      1.
      2.
      3.
   D. Third paragraph (specific information, direct quotes, etc.)
      1.
      2.
      3.

III. Headline for the News Article

5.8 Conferencing for Conventions: Newspaper Article

I. Type of Article _____

   A. Who

   B. What

   C. Where

   D. When

   E. Why

   F. How

II. Lead Sentence and Paragraph

   A. Place stars by items in Roman numeral I to indicate which of the 5 Ws and How were included in the lead sentence.

   B. What other important information is included in the lead paragraph?
     1.
     2.
     3.

   C. Second paragraph?
     1.
     2.
     3.

   D. Third paragraph?
     1.
     2.
     3.

III. What Is the Headline for the News Article? _____

_____

Does the headline reflect the news article? _____

IV. Does the News Article Make Sense? _____

What could use more information? _____

_____

I didn't understand . . . _____

I thought _____ was really good.

chapter 6

Supplementary Materials

Communication between teacher and parents is essential to involving the family within the literacy process. Therefore, this chapter includes information on supplementary resources that may be used in conjunction with the units. By sending home information pertaining to what is being studied, parents are encouraged to talk to their children about ongoing classroom activities. Since all parents are not able to participate in their children's learning during school time, this means of communication becomes a way to encourage parent involvement during the time after school or on weekends. Formats include student and parent letters, newsletters, pamphlets, and postcards, as well as student awards that can be used at the completion of the unit.

Folktale: Student Letter

Dear _____ ,

    Our class is beginning a study of folktales this week, and you are invited to embark on a treasure hunt as we learn all about this type of story. In your treasure hunt, you are to find stories representing the following:

- A story that involves a character undergoing a long sleep or enchantment.

  Title _____

  Author _____ Summary of story _____

  _____

  _____

  _____

  _____

- A story where magical powers help the character to obtain a goal.

  Title _____

  Author _____ Summary of story _____

  _____

  _____

  _____

  _____

- A folktale where a magic object helps the character to outwit another character.

  Title _____

  Author _____ Summary of story _____

  _____

  _____

  _____

- A story where the character abuses the wishes that are given to him or her.

  Title _____

  Author _____ Summary of story _____

  _____

  _____

  _____

(Continued)

■ A story where the use of trickery is used on a character.

Title _____

Author _____ Summary of story _____

_____

_____

_____

Some of these stories may be found in the classroom library, but you may also have to search in the school library, too. Be sure to include in the summary of the story the reasons why that story fits that requirement of the treasure hunt. At the end of our study, student awards to successful explorers will be passed out.

Good luck on your search, and happy hunting!!

Folktale: Parent Letter

Dear Parents,

    We are studying folktales over the next couple of weeks, and you are invited to share with us as we learn about this type of story. It would be great if you could read and talk about a folktale every night or whenever you have a chance to do so. Your child can check out a book from our classroom library, or you could visit the local library to check out books together. Ways you could work with your child include reading aloud together, rereading the same folktale on several different nights, taking turns reading aloud together, and being sure to talk about what happened in the story. Some characteristics that many folktales have in common are a very simple and easy to follow storyline, the use of magic is sometimes present, characters are either good or bad, and numbers, phrases, chants, or poems may sometimes be repeated throughout the story. After reading the story, you could also discuss together which of the characteristics were found.

    In addition, we will be trying our hand at writing, involving what we learn about folktales. Your child may choose to transform a story into a more modern version, or write letters with another student by talking and acting like one of the characters in the story. We are also having a treasure hunt, where students look for stories representing different elements found with the tale.

    Please let me know if you would like to join us or if you need help finding books to read together at home.

Fable: Parent and Student Letter

Dear _____ ,

    We will be studying fables (the next few weeks, during the school year), and you are invited to work together to find modern-day events that represent the morals from different stories we will be reading. Use resources such as newspapers, television and radio broadcasts, magazines, or home experiences to find examples. For example, "Easier said than done" can be applied to suggestions that are sometimes made by others. Suggestions to remedy the national budget or world peace are often made, but it is entirely another thing for solutions to be readily applied. Please let me know if I can help in any way. Good Luck!!

▪ Slow and steady wins the race.
   What did you find to represent this moral?

_____

_____

_____

_____

_____

▪ Some things are better small.
   What did you find to represent this moral?

_____

_____

_____

_____

_____

▪ It is the high and mighty who have the longest distance to fall.
   What did you find to represent this moral?

_____

_____

_____

_____

_____

(Continued)

■ There are those who pretend to despise what they cannot obtain.
What did you find to represent this moral?

_____

_____

_____

_____

_____

■ Even the smallest of us can do big things.
What did you find to represent this moral?

_____

_____

_____

_____

_____

Legend: Parent and Student Letter

Dear _____ ,

   We will be studying legends over the next few weeks, and you are invited to read and share with your child at home some of the legends we will be reading in class. Books are available for checkout from our classroom library, but I encourage you to visit the local library to check out these stories, too. Some popular legends include:

Tomie DePaola's *The Legend of the Indian Paintbrush*
Tomie DePaola's *The Legend of the Bluebonnet*
Olaf Baker's *Where the Buffalo Roam*
Paul Goble's *Buffalo Woman*
Ann Grifalconi's *The Village of Round and Square Houses*
Selina Hasting's *Sir Gawain and the Loathly Lady*
Mark Shannon's *Sir Gawain and the Green Knight*
David Wishniewski's *Golem*
Jane Yolen's *Merlin and the Dragons*

   I encourage you to read and discuss together some of these different legends. Let me know if I can be of any assistance. Thanks!!!

References

Abrahamson, R. A. (1995 March). Class notes. *Children's literature.* University of Houston.

Applebee, A. N., & Langer, J. A. (1984). Instructional scaffolding: Reading and writing as natural language activities. In J. M. Jensen (Ed.), *Composing and comprehending* (pp. 183–190). Urbana, IL: ERIC Clearinghouse on Reading and Communication Skills and National Conference on Research in English.

Atwell, N. (1987). *In the middle: Writing, reading, and learning with adolescents.* Portsmouth, NH: Heinemann.

Avery, C. (1993). *And with a light touch: Learning about reading, writing, and teaching with first graders.* Portsmouth, NH: Heinemann.

Barr, R., & Johnson, B. (1997). *Teaching reading and writing in elementary classrooms.* New York: Longman.

Bosma, B. (1987). *Folktales, fables, legends, and myths: Using folk literature in your classroom.* New York: Teachers College Press.

Brown, M. (1990). *Newspaper reporters: An introduction to newspaper writing.* Huntington Beach, CA: Teacher Created Materials.

Carroll, J. A. (1982). Ratiocination and revision of clues in the written draft. *The English Journal, 71,* 90–92.

Dixon-Krauss, J. (1996). *Vygotsky in the classroom: Mediated literacy instruction and assessment.* White Plains, NY: Longman.

Downes, T., & Fatouros, C. (1995). *Learning in an electronic world: Computers and the language arts classroom.* Portsmouth, NH: Heinemann.

Fisher, B. (1991). *Joyful learning: A whole language kindergarten.* Portsmouth, NH: Heinemann.

Graves, D. H. (1994). *A fresh look at writing.* Portsmouth, NH: Heinemann.

Herrell, A. L., & Fowler, J. P. (1998). *Camcorder in the classroom: Using the videocamera to enliven curriculum.* Upper Saddle River, NJ: Prentice-Hall.

Huck, C. S., Hepler, S., & Hickman, J. (1987). *Children's literature in the elementary school.* New York: Holt, Rinehart and Winston.

Macon, J. M., Bewell, D., & Vogt, M. E. (1991). *Responses to literature.* Newark, DE: IRA.

Moline, S. (1995). *I see what you mean: Children at work with visual information.* York, ME: Stenhouse.

Reutzel, D. R., & Cooter, R. B. (1996). *Teaching children to read: From basals to books.* Englewood Hills, NJ: Prentice-Hall.

Rief, L. (1992). *Seeking diversity: Language arts with adolescents.* Portsmouth, NH: Heinemann.

Rosenblatt, L. M. (1994). The transactional theory of reading and writing. In R. B. Ruddell, M. R. Ruddell, & H. Singer (Eds.), *Theoretical models and processes of reading* (pp. 1057–1092). Newark, DE: IRA.

Routman, R. (1991). *Invitations: Changing as teachers and learners K–12.* Portsmouth, NH: Heinemann.

Shanahan, T. (1988). The reading-writing relationship: Seven instructional principles. *The Reading Teacher, 41,* 636–647.

Smith, F. (1983). Reading like a writer. *Language Arts, 60,* 558–567.

Stewig, J. W., & Jett-Simpson, M. (1995). *Language arts in the early childhood classroom.* Belmont, CA: Wadsworth.

Sutherland, Z. (1997). *Children and books.* New York: Longman.

Tierney, R. J., & Pearson, P. D. (1983). Toward a composing model of reading. *Language Arts, 60,* 568–580.

Tompkins, G. E. (1990). *Teaching writing: Balancing process and product.* New York: Merrill/Macmillan.

Tompkins, G. E. (1998). *Language arts: Content and teaching strategies.* Upper Saddle River, NJ: Merrill.

Tompkins, G. E., & Hoskisson, K. (1991). *Language arts: Content and teaching strategies.* New York: Merrill/Macmillan.

Tompkins, G. E., & McGee, L. M. (1993). *Teaching reading with literature.* Englewood Cliffs, NJ: Macmillan.

Vacca, J. L., Vacca, R. T., & Gove, M. K. (1995). *Reading and learning to read.* New York: HarperCollins.

Wells, D. (1995). Leading grand conversations. In N. L. Roser & M. G. Martinez (Eds.), *Book talk and beyond: Children and teachers respond to literature* (pp. 132–139). Newark, DE: IRA.

Willis, J. W., Stephens, E. C., & Matthew, K. I. (1996). *Technology, reading, and language arts.* Boston: Allyn and Bacon.

Index